MIGRATION AND ADAPTATION

Volume 43, Sage Library of Social Research

SAGE LIBRARY OF SOCIAL RESEARCH

Migration and Adaptation

Tzintzuntzan Peasants in Mexico City

ROBERT V. KEMPER

Volume 43
SAGE LIBRARY OF
SOCIAL RESEARCH

 **SAGE PUBLICATIONS**   Beverly Hills   London

For information address:

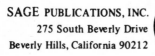

SAGE PUBLICATIONS, INC.
275 South Beverly Drive
Beverly Hills, California 90212

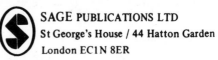

SAGE PUBLICATIONS LTD
St George's House / 44 Hatton Garden
London EC1N 8ER

Printed in the United States of America

Library of Congress Cataloging in Publication Data

Kemper, Robert V   1945–
    Migration and adaptation.

    (Sage library of social research ; v. 43)
    Includes bibliographical references.
    1. Tarasco Indians—Urban residence. 2. Indians of
Mexico—Urban residence. 3. Mexico (City)—Social
conditions. 4. Tzintzuntzan, Mexico—Social conditions.
I. Title.
F1221.T3K45   301.36'1   77-2413
ISBN 0-8039-0687-0
ISBN 0-8039-0688-9 pbk.

FIRST PRINTING

TABLE OF CONTENTS

Chapter

TABLE OF CONTENTS (*Cont.*)

FIGURES

FIGURES (*Cont.*)

TABLES

TABLES *(Cont.)*

PREFACE

This study, which developed out of my interest in peasant adaptations to Mexican modernization, combines the results of twenty months of fieldwork, between March 1969 and August 1976, with analysis of census and ethnographic data gathered by Professor George M. Foster in the course of his long-term field research in Tzintzuntzan. Not only have I drawn heavily upon his wealth of knowledge about Tzintzuntzan and its people, I also have benefited tremendously from the esteem, trust, and respect he has earned from villagers and migrants alike. His active encouragement and support of my research is reflected throughout this volume, especially in Chapter One, which is derived in large part from our joint paper (Kemper and Foster 1975) previously published in the Sage *Latin American Urban Research* series.

In this volume I focus on migration and adaptation. Most social scientists are comfortable with "migration" as an analytical category, but some distrust "adaptation" as being too vague or too much like assimilation, adjustment, or acculturation. My preference for the term "adaptation" sums up "a growing consensus among anthropologists that the nature of man is best described as neither totally active nor passive but interactive. Operating within the many constraints which his physical and social environments impose, he seeks to overcome the problems confronting him by choosing among perceived available options" (Graves and Graves 1974:117). In my view, the act of migration represents one adaptation to traditional peasant life in Mexican villages; being successful in the urban setting represents another aspect of adaptation to the forces of modernization.

This volume attempts to follow a particular population through the temporal-spatial process of migration and adaptation and, therefore, will probably dissatisfy those who prefer a full-fledged treatment of all migrants' (and natives') interaction with the Mexican urban system. I do not apologize for emphasizing a case study approach. As Cornelius, a political scientist, has pointed out, "the *anthropological approach* to urban studies is particularly well suited to answering a variety of key questions about cities and the urbanization process in Latin America and other developing regions. One of the major strengths of the anthropological approach grows out of its deep concern for what happens at the grass-roots level of society" (1974:10). Moreover, through the case study methodology employed here, it becomes possible to analyze the interaction of rural and urban areas within the overall process of modernization. The point of origin and the place of destination are both known to a degree not possible in broader, cross-sectional sample survey approaches to the study of cityward migration. Thus, we can deal with adaptation as the interaction of people with their social and physical environments both before and after migration.

This leads to a necessary *caveat*. Because migration and adaptation are complex spatial and temporal processes, best suited to analysis over a full generation or more, the present volume represents only an initial report on my research. The advantage of a longitudinal perspective is an awareness that unanticipated changes occur in the social and physical environments in which migrants operate. For instance, the Mexican government's recent decision to devalue the peso from the long-standing rate of 12.5 to the dollar—the figure used throughout this volume—to a new rate of about 22 to 24 pesos to the dollar may have important consequences for the migrants in Mexico City.

The geographical dispersion of Tzintzuntzeños in Mexico City has proven to be a significant constraint on the research. Because the migrants are not settled in a single neighborhood or zone of the metropolis, I have already travelled more than 10,000 miles—by automobile, bus, and subway—to find them, to interview them, and to observe their daily routines. On a typical day I might drive up to 50 miles, make several visits, and set up future appointments; but, all too often, I drove across the city only to find that the people were not at home or had not lived at that address for some time. Thus, I felt that my experience simulated in some ways those of the Tzintzuntzan migrants who settled in Mexico City. Just as they had done before me, I started with only a few ties, slowly built up a substantial network of friends and acquaintances, and found that my interaction with most Tzintzuntzeños in the city was severely limited by our geographical separation from each other.

This study has been possible because of the friendly cooperation of the people of Tzintzuntzan—who are given pseudonymns in this volume—and the many useful comments I have received from social scientists in Mexico and the United States. In particular, I wish to thank May N. Diaz and William P. McGreevey, who served with Foster on my dissertation committee at the University of California (Berkeley). Others who have materially contributed to the ideas expressed here include: Harley Browning, Douglas Butterworth, Fernando Cámara, Wayne Cornelius, Henry Dietz, Theodore Downing, Anthony Leeds, Larissa Lomnitz, Angel Palerm, Jack Rollwagen, Anya Peterson Royce, Lyle Shannon, Alex Stepick, Claudio Stern, Alfonso Villa Rojas, Douglas Uzzell, Thomas Weaver, Michael Whiteford, Scott Whiteford, and Richard Wilkie. I look forward to their evaluation of this volume and their suggestions for my continuing fieldwork among the Tzintzuntzan migrants. I would also like to acknowledge the support of my colleagues in the Department of Anthropology at Southern Methodist University and the institutional cooperation kindly provided to me in Mexico by the Instituto Nacional de Antropología e Historia, the Instituto Nacional Indigenista, the Colegio de México, the Instituto Indigenista Interamericano, and the Universidad Ibero-Americana.

The initial research for this study was made possible by a traineeship (No. GM-1224) in anthropology from the Division of General Medical Sciences of the National Institutes of Health administered by the Department of Anthropology, University of California (Berkeley). Additional financial support was received from the Center for Latin American Studies, University of California (Berkeley) for the months of July to September 1971 and from the Wenner-Gren Foundation for Anthropological Research, Inc., for the summer of 1974. The Wenner-Gren Foundation subsequently provided an additional grant which permitted me to return to the field in August 1976 and to assemble my ethnographic materials for this volume. The unusually large number of illustrations was possible only because of the Foundation's generous financial support. In recognition of their assistance, I have arranged for the publisher to provide, in lieu of the usual royalties, a supply of copies of this volume at no charge for interested non-U.S. Associates of *Current Anthropology*.

Two special debts remain to be mentioned. First, I owe more than I can say to Natalie Kern, Donna Osgood, Kelly Platte Seibel, and Winifred Vass of SMU's ISEM Graphics Lab for their extraordinary dedication in typesetting, editing, and producing the camera-ready copy for this book. Linda Verrett did the maps; I am responsible for the photographs. Secretarial assistance was provided by Shirley Bailey, Hazel Gilboe, and Shirley King of the SMU Department of Anthropology. Finally, I wish to acknowledge my appreciation for the continuing support I receive from my wife, Sandra, whose perceptive observations, assistance, and encouragement have significantly contributed to my research among the Tzintzuntzan migrants.

CHAPTER 1

THE MODERNIZATION OF TZINTZUNTZAN

INTRODUCTION

This study deals with a microcosm of Mexican urbanization: emigration from the traditional peasant village of Tzintzuntzan, Michoacán, located on the shores of Lake Pátzcuaro, 400 kilometers west of Mexico City. Prior to World War II, few Tzintzuntzeños ventured far from their natal community. The Mexican Revolution of 1910 disrupted local life far less than in other parts of the country and produced no refugee group. Out-migration during the period between the two wars was limited, and only with the beginning of the *bracero* program early in World War II, when large numbers of Mexican field hands were contracted for agricultural work in the United States, did significant numbers of villagers venture far from home. This program, which continued until the end of 1964, took almost half of all adult Tzintzuntzan males at least once to the United States, and many made a dozen or more trips, sometimes legally and sometimes illegally. Although a hard-surfaced road, electricity, and potable water came to Tzintzuntzan in the late 1930s, this migration experience seems primarily responsible for opening the eyes of the villagers to the possibilities of the wider world. When the bracero program ended, the village was accustomed to relatively large infusions of outside income—its limited resources, in the face of a rapidly growing population, were inadequate to meet even minimal human needs. Consequently, since 1965 increasing numbers of people are turning to Mexican cities—and particularly Mexico City—to find alternate sources of employment.

For at least two reasons Tzintzuntzan is especially well suited for a microcosmic study of the emigration process. On

FIG. 1-1—View of Tzintzuntzan and Lake Pátzcuaro (looking west).

the one hand, since the bulk of the emigration is recent, we can deal with real people, and not simply with statistics. And these people are known, as are their families, their socio-economic status, and their histories, to an extent not normally the case, since a thorough study of the village was made during the period 1944-1946 (Foster and Ospina 1948). Since 1958, the community has been the object of a continuing long-term study, which includes complete ethnographic censuses in 1960 and 1970 (Foster 1967). As a result, the raw materials for examining emigration are of exceptional quantity and quality.

HISTORY AND POPULATION GROWTH

Although today Tzintzuntzan is, and appears always to have been, a typical Mexican village, appearances are deceiving. At the time of the Spanish Conquest of Mexico it was the capital of the Tarascan Indian Empire, which included most of the modern state of Michoacán and adjoining areas—an empire which successfully withstood the Aztecs. After the Conquest, its eminence was short-lived. Don Vasco de Quiroga, first Bishop of Michoacán, established his bishopric here, but after only a year he realized the geographical limitations of the site and in 1540 transfered the bishopric to Pátzcuaro, ten miles to the south. Subsequently it was moved to a new city, Valladolid, which became Morelia after Independence. The Franciscan monastery, established soon after the city was taken by Spaniards in 1525, functioned until the 1770s; but for the past two centuries, almost nothing has distinguished the village, apart from its fame for superior pottery and the richness of its ceremonial life.

During the four centuries following the Conquest, the village's population appears to have been stable, fluctuating around 1,000 persons. A high birth rate was balanced by a high death rate, while limited in-migration from nearby hamlets seems to have just about matched out-migration. Resources, although limited, were apparently sufficient to meet the simple subsistence requirements of peasants who knew no other way of life (Foster 1967:264).

Then, beginning in the late 1930s, and gaining momentum in the 1940s and 1950s, Tzintzuntzan's population underwent a dramatic change. This transformation is confirmed through two different sets of census data. The Mexican government census shows that the village grew from 1,003 persons in 1930 to 1,077 in 1940–1,336 in 1950–1,840 in 1960–and 2,196 in 1970. This means that the population increased 0.7% per annum between 1930 and 1940; 2.1% per annum between 1940 and 1950; 3.2% per annum between 1950 and 1960; and 1.6% per annum between 1960 and 1970. The ethnographic censuses conducted by Foster reveal that Tzintzuntzan had 1,231 persons in 1945–1,877 in 1960–and 2,253 in 1970. Using the 1930 figure of 1,003 as a baseline, Foster's data suggest that the population grew at a rate of 1.4% per annum from 1930 to 1945, 2.8% per annum from 1945 to 1960, and 1.8% per annum from 1960 to 1970. Both data sets, therefore, provide strong evidence that Tzintzuntzan has passed through its period of most rapid population expansion, at least as this is measured by its *resident* population.

The population profiles for 1945, 1960, and 1970 illustrated in Table 1-1 and Fig. 1-2 reveal the extent to which Tzintzuntzan's demographic structure has been transformed in the span of a generation. The interaction of natural and social factors has had profound impact on all age-sex cohorts from the children to the village elders. Examination of the crude death and birth rates for Tzintzuntzan and the Mexican nation as a whole (Table 1-2) shows that the net population increase in the village was well below the national norm for the 1935-1945 period, but has approached the norm in recent years. It should be obvious that the decline in mortality has been a major contributor to the village population growth in concert with a smaller, but still significant, decline in the crude birth rate since the 1950s. The effect of migration has been most important since the mid-1960s and has primarily involved the middle sectors of the village's age-sex cohorts. (The various aspects of emigration from Tzintzuntzan will be discussed in detail in Chapter 2.)

THE ECONOMIC SITUATION

Tzintzuntzan's population growth has not occurred in a vacuum. The traditional way of life also has changed for the great majority of the villagers. Turning first to the local occupational structure, we see from the figures in Table 1-3 that pottery-making continues to be the primary occupation of most household heads. It has, however, declined in relative importance as potters' sons and daughters abandon the craft for commerce and day labor—or leave the village altogether to seek their fortune elsewhere. The percentage of farmers and fishermen has also declined during the past three decades. Land continues to be in short supply, and the increased population has created added pressures on a limited supply of good agricultural properties. At the same time, severe over-fishing of the lake combined with an infestation of water lillies has so decreased fishing prospects that by 1974 only a single Tzintzuntzeño still derived his primary income from this activity.

While these occupations have declined in importance, the number of day laborers has greatly increased, as have the numbers of employees and "miscellaneous" workers. The "employee" category includes Tzintzuntzeños working in the local schools; in the village's small clinic; and in various posts with the local, municipal, and state government agencies based in the community. The "miscellaneous" category includes the growing group of specialists such as bakers, butchers, and refreshment stand operators. And although

TABLE 1-1
Age-Sex Profile for Tzintzuntzan

Age Cohort	1945				1960				1970			
	Male	Female	Total	%	Male	Female	Total	%	Male	Female	Total	%
86+	nd	nd	nd	nd	1	3	4	0.2	1	1	2	0.1
81-85	0	1	1	0.1	1	3	4	0.2	2	2	4	0.2
76-80	2	2	4	0.3	4	2	6	0.3	6	7	13	0.6
71-75	1	4	5	0.4	6	7	13	0.7	13	10.	23	1.0
66-70	8	8	16	1.3	16	11	27	1.4	34	25	59	2.6
61-65	10	10	20	1.6	9	19	28	1.5	24	30	54	2.4
56-60	18	18	36	2.9	27	21	48	2.6	25	22	47	2.1
51-55	19	13	32	2.6	31	34	65	3.5	24	25	49	2.2
46-50	22	37	59	4.8	32	37	69	3.7	43	49	92	4.1
41-45	32	39	71	5.8	36	28	64	3.4	44	46	90	4.0
36-40	48	43	91	7.4	53	55	108	5.7	58	61	119	5.3
31-35	29	41	70	5.7	36	49	85	4.5	44	58	102	4.5
26-30	41	43	84	6.8	51	63	114	6.1	58	75	133	5.9
21-25	56	54	110	8.9	80	72	152	8.1	71	79	150	6.6
16-20	60	65	125	10.2	68	114	182	9.7	122	112	234	10.4
11-15	57	79	136	11.0	127	107	234	12.5	128	152	280	12.4
6-10	84	88	172	14.0	156	144	300	16.0	185	189	374	16.6
0-5	82	117	199	16.2	168	206	374	19.9	222	206	428	19.0
Total	569	662	1,231	100.0	902	975	1,877	100.0	1,104	1,149	2,253	100.0

Sources: For 1945, Foster and Ospina 1948:28 (Table 1); for 1960, Foster 1967:36; for 1970, analysis of Foster's unpublished ethnographic census materials.

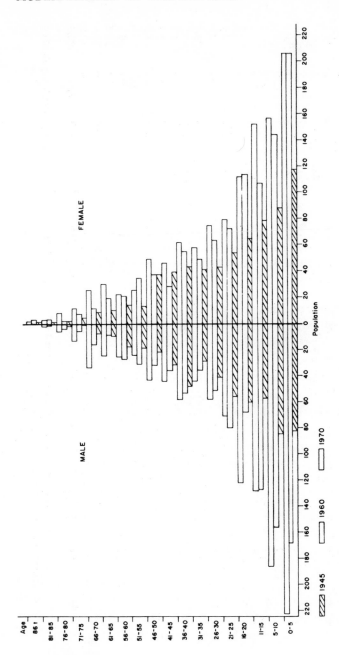

FIG. 1-2–Age-Sex Pyramid for Tzintzuntzan: 1945, 1960, and 1970.

TABLE 1-2
Birth and Death Rates: Tzintzuntzan and Mexico

Decade centered on:	1940	1950	1960	1970
Tzintzuntzan[1]				
Birth Rate per 1,000	46.8	50.7	44.1	39.0
Death Rate per 1,000	29.8	16.8	8.7	8.3
Net Increase	17.0	33.9	35.4	30.7
Mexico[2]				
Birth Rate per 1,000	48.1	46.3	44.9	41.3
Death Rate per 1,000	22.6	15.9	11.3	9.2
Net Increase	25.5	30.4	33.6	32.1

Sources: [1] For Tzintzuntzan, 1940-1960, Foster 1967:265; for 1970, analysis of Foster's unpublished ethnographic archives; [2] For Mexico, 1940-1960, C.E.E.D. 1970:8 (Table I-2); for 1970, United Nations 1971:120 (Table 3).

their numbers had not grown dramatically by 1970, the impact of pottery resellers on village life also has been substantial. These middlemen traditionally took mules laden with local goods to the *tierra caliente* where they exchanged these goods for cheeses, dried meats, and other products of the lowlands. Today, local middlemen travel in the latest model pick-ups and half-ton trucks to the northern border cities where they sell substantial quantities of pottery and other craft products at considerable profits.

The past three decades have also meant rising standards of living for most households in Tzintzuntzan. In 1945, when the first ethnographic census was taken, many families still lived in houses little different from those their ancestors had inhabited several generations earlier. The contemporary contrast with the village of 1945 is obvious from the figures in Table 1-4 and Table 1-5. Aside from the raised hearth, a great convenience to a tortilla maker, most items listed have been introduced fairly recently. Progress has not been limited to house improvements; increasing numbers of villagers compete to be first, or among the first, to possess and display con-

TABLE 1-3
Occupational Structure in Tzintzuntzan

Occupation	1945			1960			1970		
	No.	%	Rank	No.	%	Rank	No.	%	Rank
Potter	118	48.0	1	167	52.1	1	167	46.4	1
Farmer	37	15.0	2	39	12.2	2	27	7.5	4
Pottery Reseller[a]	26	10.6	3	14	4.4	5	17	4.7	5
Day Laborer	20	8.1	4	37	11.6	3	53	14.7	2
Housekeeper	13	5.3	5	10	3.1	7	13	3.6	8
Fisherman	8	3.3	6	16	5.0	4	13	3.6	8
Miscellaneous	8	3.3	6	14	4.4	5	34	9.4	3
Construction	7	2.8	8	8	2.5	9	5	1.4	10
Storekeeper	5	2.0	9	5	1.6	10	14	3.9	7
Employee	4	1.6	10	10	3.1	7	17	4.7	5
Totals[b]	246	100.0		320	100.0		360	100.0	

[a]For 1945, "pottery reseller" means muleteer (*arriero*); for 1960 and 1970, "pottery reseller" means persons who own pottery stands or trucks.

[b]The "totals" represent the primary occupation of household heads only; they do not include other workers nor do they include secondary jobs held by household heads.

Sources: All data are derived from analysis of Foster's unpublished ethnographic census materials.

TABLE 1-4
Household Improvements in Tzintzuntzan

Item	1945		1960		1970	
	N	%	N	%	N	%
Raised Hearth	148[a]	60.0[a]	240	75.0	266	73.9
Patio Water Tap	54	22.0	152	47.5	230	63.9
Latrine	47	19.1	137	42.8	202	56.1
Electricity	35	14.2	156	48.8	232	64.4
Whitewashed Exterior	n.d.[b]	–	148	46.2	159	44.2
Hard Floor	n.d.[b]	–	106	33.1	139	38.6
3 Rooms or More	87	35.4	104	32.5	194	53.9
Glass Window	n.d.[b]	–	15	4.7	50	13.9
Shower Bath	0	0.0	2	0.6	14	3.9
Flush Toilet	0	0.0	0	0.0	4	1.1

[a]Estimated total and percentage; [b]n.d. = no data available.

Sources: Figures for 1945 [N = 246] are derived from Foster and Ospina
1948:38; figures for 1960 [N = 320] and 1970 [N = 360] from analysis of
Foster's unpublished ethnographic census materials.

sumer goods once unknown on the local scene. As a result,
many homes now have amenities usually associated with
the urban middle class—including gas stoves, innerspring
mattresses, television sets, stereo consoles, radios, electric
blenders, flush toilets, and even automatic washing machines.

The recent improvement in standard of living is particularly evident from the comparison of quartile distributions
for village homes in 1960 and 1970 given in Table 1-6. But
even these data do not fully reflect the situation today. For
example, in 1972 the Federal Commission of Electricity extended its lines to peripheral parts of Tzintzuntzan, for the
first time making electricity available to *all* homes. In the
extreme western *barrio*, "El Rincón," 22 of the 27 home
owners promptly signed up. Today the percentage of village
subscribers to electrical service is probably between 85% and

TABLE 1-5
Major Consumer Goods in Tzintzuntzan

Item	1945 N	1945 %	1960 N	1960 %	1970 N	1970 %
Raised Bed	143	58.1	221	69.1	268	74.4
Radio	20[a]	8.1[a]	124	38.8	242	67.2
Electric Iron	0	0.0	100	31.2	156	43.3
Sewing Machine	15[a]	6.1[a]	60	18.8	63	17.5
Store-bought Mattress	8	3.2	53	16.6	73	20.3
Stove:						
a) propane gas	0	0.0	0	0.0	50	13.9
b) kerosene	0	0.0	0	0.0	16	4.4
Television Set	0	0.0	0	0.0	37	10.3
Electric Blender	0	0.0	0	0.0	17	4.7
Automobile/Truck	0	0.0	1	0.3	11	3.1
Automatic Washing Machine	0	0.0	0	0.0	5	1.4

[a]Estimated totals and percentages.

Sources: Figures for 1945 [N = 246] are derived from Foster and Ospina 1948:
38; figures for 1960 [N = 320] and 1970 [N = 360] from analysis of Foster's
unpublished ethnographic census materials.

90 percent. Similarly, the number of television sets has grown
dramatically in the past four years. There were only 37 in
1970, and now there are well over 100! The number of gas
stoves also has risen considerably since the 1970 census, with
the current figure close to 100. Perhaps the most impressive
measure of recent progress, however, is the increase in motor
vehicles owned by Tzintzuntzeños. By 1974 there were five
big vans, two light VW vans, ten pick-up trucks, and seven
passenger cars—a total of 32 vehicles in all, and the number is
still growing.

The intra-village disparities in living conditions resulting
from this progress means that the local saying "here we are
all equal" ceases to describe accurately the reality of village
life. One measure of increasing wealth differentiation in Tzin-

TABLE 1-6
Standard of Living in Tzintzuntzan

	1960			1970			
Scale Score	N	%	Cum. %	N	%	Cum. %	Quartiles
30	0	0.0	100.0	0	0.0	100.0	
29	0	0.0	100.0	0	0.0	100.0	
28	0	0.0	100.0	2	0.6	100.0	
27	0	0.0	100.0	0	0.0	99.4	
26	0	0.0	100.0	3	0.8	99.4	
25	0	0.0	100.0	3	0.8	98.6	
24	0	0.0	100.0	5	1.4	97.8	
23	0	0.0	100.0	2	0.6	96.4	IV
22	2	0.6	100.0	6	1.7	95.8	
21	1	0.3	99.4	6	1.7	94.1	
20	4	1.2	99.1	4	1.1	92.4	
19	4	1.2	97.9	8	2.2	91.3	
18	11	3.4	96.7	13	3.6	89.1	
17	11	3.4	93.3	22	6.1	85.5	
16	13	4.1	89.9	15	4.2	79.4	
15	15	4.7	85.8	18	5.0	75.2	
14	10	3.1	81.1	18	5.0	70.2	
13	14	4.4	78.0	16	4.4	65.2	
12	14	4.4	73.6	19	5.3	60.8	III
11	15	4.7	69.2	23	6.4	55.5	
10	16	5.0	64.5	25	7.0	49.1	
9	14	4.4	59.5	12	3.3	42.1	
8	17	5.3	55.1	14	3.9	38.8	
7	19	5.9	49.8	18	5.0	34.9	II
6	21	6.6	43.9	17	4.7	29.9	
5	15	4.7	37.3	22	6.1	25.2	
4	24	7.5	32.6	20	5.6	19.1	
3	8	2.5	25.1	8	2.2	13.5	
2	35	11.0	22.6	21	5.8	11.3	
1	7	2.2	11.6	4	1.1	5.5	I
0	30	9.4	9.4	16	4.4	4.4	
Total	320	100.0		360	100.0		
Mean		8.3			10.8		
S.D.		5.8			6.4		

tzuntzan is that most of the best homes are now located on or near the main plaza or along the highway through the town's center, whereas the poorest are found on the outskirts, either west in El Rincón or east in Yahuaro.

Nevertheless, changes in living standards in Tzintzuntzan are not irreversible: few villagers are secure enough to weather a severe economic recession, particularly since the demand for local pottery and the prices which must be paid for consumer goods and services are determined externally by forces beyond local control.

EDUCATIONAL PROGRESS

Unlike many rural Mexican villages, Tzintzuntzan has long had its own school, with a three-year primary program as early as 1869. However, attendance was sporadic because most parents believed education of little value to success as a potter, farmer, or fisherman. Even the construction of a fine, new school building in 1939, through the efforts of President Lázaro Cárdenas, instilled only temporary enthusiasm for education. The high drop-out rate for the fourth, fifth, and sixth grades during the 1940s and 1950s is clear from these figures: registration from 1940 to 1959 averaged between 175 and 200 students per year, but only 92 children grad-

---

Note: The 30-point Standard of Living Index combines household improvements and major consumer goods. It consists of the following items (each of which is given with its weight in the index): *Household Improvements*–raised hearth (2); patio water tap (2); latrine (2); electricity (2); whitewashed exterior (1); glass window (1); shower bath (2); flush toilet (1); *Major Consumer Goods*–raised bed (2); radio (1); electric iron (1); sewing machine (1); store-bought mattress (1); stove [propane (2), kerosene (1)]; television set (2); electric blender (1); automobile/truck (2); automatic washing machine (1).

Source: Analysis of unpublished census data collected by Foster in 1960 and 1970.

uated from sixth grade during this period. In fact, no class graduated for eleven of the twenty years, and the largest number of graduates was fifteen in 1947.

In the 1960s, however, most Tzintzuntzeños acquired a new interest in education. Local primary school registration is higher than ever and more children entering the first grade now finish sixth grade. The school's physical plant was replaced by prefabricated modular units in 1970 because the old buildings had so deteriorated during thirty years of use and misuse.

Moreover, the villagers have cooperated to an unprecedented extent to establish a secondary school program in Tzintzuntzan. Started on a trial basis in September 1974, the secondary school began with 56 students in the first year program and had 95 students in 1975-76 school year in the first and second year programs. The final third year of the program was added for the 1976-77 academic year. Currently, the school is recognized by the government as "private," but local parents and children hope to have it "federalized" soon. This would mean that the teachers' salaries and other physical plant costs would be borne by the government and would therefore reduce the direct cost to the villagers. They now pay 80 pesos/month for each child enrolled in the school, a figure still half that required to send a student to secondary school in nearby Pátzcuaro.

Because of the high cost of sending children to outside secondary schools and because of the lack of interest among Tzintzuntzeños in higher education in earlier years, only 19 village children had ever attended secondary school prior to 1960. Today, from 75 to 100 are currently enrolled in outside secondary schools, preparatories, normal schools, seminaries, and universities. In fact, of the 325 village children who completed sixth grade between 1960 and 1970, more than 100 have continued their studies. This dramatic increase in schooling is reflected in the rising literacy rate in Tzintzuntzan. In 1945 only 53% of household heads could read and write, and this figure improved only slightly—to 58%—by 1960. In contrast, the literacy rate climbed to 70.3% in 1970, and today it probably has reached 75%.

Education also provides a popular career for many of Tzintzuntzan's young people. To become a school teacher is the most common and most realistic goal of many bright young students. From 1945 to 1970, some 30 villagers became state or federal school teachers. Since 1970, another 30 have been added to the rolls! Indeed, after pottery and other crafts, school teachers are one of Tzintzuntzan's principal contributions to Mexican development.

WORLDVIEW TRANSFORMATION

Changes in population, shifts in occupational categories, improvements in living standards, and progress in education are all relatively easy to document in Tzintzuntzan's recent history. Changes in values, attitudes, and aspirations are much more difficult to assess. Some, such as a changed appreciation for schooling, are fairly obvious; and in this domain it is clear that the village has undergone a revolution during the past 15 years. Other changes can be inferred from close observation of the daily activities of Tzintzuntzeños. For instance, a "time-is-money" attitude is evidenced by a recent shift to buying tortillas rather than making them at home. Although the villagers recognize that machine-made tortillas are inferior to the hand-made variety, a majority of families now rely on *tortillerías* for their everyday supply. This allows women increased time for more productive work, which may include pottery-making, store-keeping, day labor, or commerce in arts and crafts.

Most striking of all the recent cultural changes in Tzintzuntzan is the breakdown of the traditional zero-sum game mentality that served to discourage innovation and modernization for many years. This cognitive orientation, labeled "the image of limited good" by Foster (1965), was calculated to maintain the status quo, and it was based on four major premises (Foster 1972:58-59):

(a) A normative individual behavior that minimizes the settings or situations in which ego may be exploited by others, i.e., rise at his expense, is preferred. This behavior stresses the avoidance of close ties with others (unless validated by ritual safeguards), distrust, and concealment or denial of "good" possessed. The individual is confronted with a prisoner's dilemma payoff matrix in which cooperative urges are discouraged by the recognition that such action can be exploited by the other player, to ego's detriment.

(b) Violations of the preferred normative behavior are discouraged by invidious sanctions such as gossip, backbiting, witchcraft, and assault.

(c) Achieved or threatened power and wealth imbalances are neutralized through redistributive (or siphon) mechanisms such as fiestas and other forms of ritual hospitality.

(d) Acquisition of additional good is permitted (but not encouraged) by tapping sources outside the system: finding treasure, winning on the lottery, obtaining human and supernatural patrons (including pacts with the Devil), and working for wages beyond the boundaries of the system. Since such "good" clearly is not at the expense of others, it is "safe," and can be permitted without threatening the stability of the system.

Only in recent years have more than a handful of Tzintzuntzeños been willing to confront and reject the traditional worldview. As early as 1965 Foster noted the appearance of people who competed openly for status and prestige through acquisition of material possessions and through visible house improvements (like constructing a second story). This tendency continues at an accelerated rate, and increasing numbers of villagers display their economic progress without fearing the envy of less successful neighbors. As a result, the "image of limited good" is being replaced by an "image of unlimited good." Tzintzunteños no longer treat the local system *as if* it existed in isolation from the national and international scene. And they perceive that progress within this larger system is possible without harming their fellow villagers' opportunities to get ahead.

This transformation of worldview is not, however, a simple, one-way process. People oscillate between the old and the new rather than commit themselves wholly to the unknown. The opening up of Tzintzuntzan's world means that villagers must recognize and cope with risks formerly beyond their experience. The ways in which Tzintzunteños deal with this new situation represent a key element in their modernization. Those who refuse to change from traditional modes of behavior and those who see the old ways as silly and out-moded provide the poles of a continuum of responses in which the rest of the villagers can be placed.

As just one example of the transition from tradition to modernity, consider the case of a young woman who sometimes works in the capital as a domestic servant but who normally lives in Tzintzuntzan with her husband and children. Several informants pointed out that this woman is highly adaptable: when she comes to the city she wears a miniskirt, fashionable shoes, and has her hair styled high up on the head. When she is in the village she prefers to walk barefoot and wear traditional Indian dress. The informants have even given her a nickname, "*la polifacética*," to convey the many facets of her personality. She is like a chameleon, changing her colors to suit the background, changing her attitudes and worldviews as the situation demands. And indeed,

Tzintzuntzan is in a state of flux in which traditional be-
haviors are giving way—sometimes grudgingly—to new styles,
values, and ideas.

THE IMPACT OF GOVERNMENTAL PROGRAMS

The first wave of governmental influences was felt in Tzintzuntzan in the 1930s. The *municipio* of Tzintzuntzan was
formed by a decree on 2 October 1930, under the governor-
ship of Lázaro Cárdenas, who "was anxious, even if only in a
symbolic way, to restore some of the vanished grandeur of
the former seat of the Tarascan Empire" (Foster and Ospina
1948:176). This municipio consists of Tzintzuntzan itself, as
cabecera, plus another 30 or so smaller settlements. Thus,
since the 1930s, the village has been a regional focus for
governmental authority, just as its parish church for centuries
has been an important religious center (see Fig. 1-3).

Infrastructure Development

Soon after the municipio was created, Cárdenas sent a Cultural Mission to Tzintzuntzan. This group consisted of
"teachers specializing in plastic arts, social work, music,
home economics, physical education, and 'small industries,'
and a nurse-midwife and an agricultural engineer" (Foster
1967:26). While the Cultural Mission produced no immediate
successes, it marked a turning point in village life. Tzintzuntzeños had their curiosity aroused, and they became less fear-
ful of outsiders.

In the wake of the Cultural Mission, and as a consequence
of Cárdenas' personal interest in Tzintzuntzan, the basic elements of a modern infrastructure began arriving. In 1938 the
first electrical lines reached the community from nearby
Pátzcuaro; running water was installed by laying iron pipes to
a nearby spring; and an iron bandstand was even brought

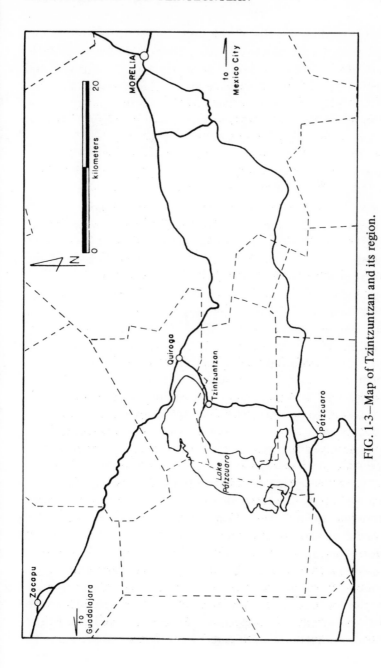

FIG. 1-3–Map of Tzintzuntzan and its region.

from the state capital to enliven the village plaza! In the following year, construction was completed on a paved highway linking Tzintzuntzan to Pátzcuaro and Quiroga, and thereby to the *tierra caliente* and to Morelia, Guadalajara, Mexico City, the rest of the nation, and the United States. Also, in 1939 the village received its first six-year federal primary school, dedicated by Cárdenas himself.

Health Care Improvements

Because of World War II, and because of the government's post-war emphasis on urban-industrial development, little more occurred in Tzintzuntzan until the mid-1950s, when the Ministry of Health offered villagers assistance in latrine and shower bath construction, instructed them in the value of cement floors, offered immunization programs and, by 1960, built a small health center staffed by a nurse-midwife and *practicante* physician. These health services, in conjunction with good access to medical facilities in Pátzcuaro, Quiroga, Morelia, and even Mexico City, have had a significant role in lowering the villagers' mortality rate. As a further result, most Tzintzuntzeños now prefer physicians to *curanderos*, and except for childhood folk diseases like "evil eye" and *empacho*, people with money for fees and medicines seek the attentions of physicians. Commenting on the relative merits of the two types of treatment, one mother in her mid-thirties laughingly remarked that when her children were sick she always took them to a physician. Only when the physician did not effect a quick cure would she turn to a curandero. This is an interesting reversal of the oft-noted pattern in which peasants turn to doctors only in desperation, after the local curers have failed. A more recent indication of the growing reliance on modern medical practitioners is that about 80% of recorded deaths now bear the name of an attending physician. Even in the mid-1960s, the figure was less than 10 percent. Government programs to improve the villagers' health have been very successful but have had the effect, presumably unintended, of increasing the local population and creating further demands for medical services that the government does not provide in rural communities. Thus, health care improvements have brought Tzintzuntzeños into more intimate contact with cities where adequate health care is available.

The Bracero Program

The government program with the greatest impact on Tzintzuntzan was created early in World War II and continued through 1964. A series of American-Mexican agreements allowed the temporary migration of farm laborers to the United States where they were contracted primarily for agricultural stoop labor in the central, south-western, and western states. During the quarter-century of the program, more than half of all Tzintzuntzan household heads worked as braceros at least once, and many men went north a number of occasions.

The social and economic consequences of this massive temporary migration have been significant and irreversible. Exposure to life styles wrought a permanent rise in aspirations as men returned to Tzintzuntzan with new consumer goods and with the economic means to improve their living conditions. The program's stimulus to Tzintzuntzan's development also included many innovations. For instance, the braceros abandoned the traditional *calzones* for jeans and jackets, and women's costly home-made wool dresses were replaced by inexpensive cotton garments produced by Mexico's growing garment industry. In addition, braceros brought in most of the village's radios during the 1940s and brought in the first television sets in the 1960s. This exposure to American life also brought in new ideas and attitudes. As Foster (1967:30) reports,

It was a bracero, and not a stay-at-home, who once astonished me by asking, "Doctor, what can we do to bring industry to Tzintzuntzan?" He had noticed the same thing another bracero had observed: "In the United States, even in little towns, like this, I saw tall smokestacks, and at the bottom of the smokestacks, lots of people were working. Here our villages have no smokestacks."

The termination of the bracero program ended a vital economic transfusion for Tzintzuntzan, a community with too few employment opportunities and too many people. Moreover, while it lasted, the program had the effect of keeping most Tzintzuntzeños tied to their homes. When it ended, many quickly saw the excellent opportunities available in Mexican cities and emigrated. The long-term impact of the bracero program is still unclear, but without question many Tzintzuntzeños achieved economic progress impossible under traditional circumstances.

Mass Communication

The Mexican government has spent millions of pesos during recent decades to create a nationwide communications system. The people of Tzintzuntzan have reaped many benefits from this policy. For a number of years villagers have been able to send and receive mail from Tzintzuntzan, but so far there is only one telephone to serve the community. It was installed in 1964 in a privately-owned store in the central plaza. Radio stations, both public and private, also help spread urban influences among the local population. In fact, the most recent "prestige" purchase is a stereo console, many of which have shortwave receivers capable of receiving the Voice of America, Armed Forces Radio Network, and stations from Europe and other Latin American nations.

The most important element of the mass communications

system is television, available to the villagers for 15 years. Tzintzuntzeños watch news programs, especially the popular 7 p.m. news and the late-night program called "24 Horas." Television, and news programs in particular, provide villagers with instant access to ideas and events that once took months or years to filter down to the Mexican countryside. For instance, in the summer of 1974 we found that many Tzintzuntzeños were familiar with the Watergate scandal. Indeed, a number of them watched Nixon's resignation speech on a live telecast dubbed into Spanish! Television is also the primary source of sports programs ranging from soccer, boxing, basketball, and American football to the more exotic Olympic sports. Through television, therefore, villagers obtain an image, sometimes distorted, of urban life which broadens their horizons, increases their aspirations, and equips them to cope with urbanites when they emigrate to the city or when they sell pottery to tourists passing through Tzintzuntzan.

Tourist Development

The natural beauty of the Lake Pátzcuaro area—and the attractions of its artisans and craftsmen—makes it one of Mexico's major tourist areas. The national and state governments have actively promoted tourism in the region, and Tzintzuntzan has received a good share of attention for its famous pottery and its traditional religious festivals (e.g., The Day of the Dead, Holy Week, and the day of the local patron saint). The government also has done much to build the reputation of village craftsmen by purchasing their best works for resale in stores run by the Banco Nacional de Fomento Cooperativo and the Instituto Nacional Indigenista. These stores are located in Mexico City, Guadalajara, Morelia, and in several northern border cities. Furthermore, in

1974, the wife of President Luis Echeverría came to Tzintzuntzan to dedicate a new colonial-style arcade where
pottery and crafts may be sold to tourists in a more "ele-
gant" setting than that provided by the adobe and wood
stands located across the street. Unfortunately, this arcade
has fallen under the control of a single family and other
villagers are upset that they are not able to obtain stalls.

Other government efforts to lure tourists to the Lake
Pátzcuaro region are having mixed effects on Tzintzuntzan.
The opening of the short-route highway from Morelia to
Pátzcuaro bypassed Quiroga and Tzintzuntzan, with the
result that many tourists headed for the famous Friday
market in Pátzcuaro no longer go through Tzintzuntzan. At
the same time, however, the state government and the
National Fine Arts Institute have provided several hundred
thousand pesos to restore Tzintzuntzan's convent and church
to its sixteenth-century stature. They are using local labor—in
itself a boon to the village economy—and are hopeful that the
restoration will attract travellers to the community. And
there is talk, as there has been for years, that the government
will finally get the Yácatas ("pyramids") fully excavated and
restored to the condition in which they were when the
Tarascan kings ruled Tzintzuntzan.

The Ejido Program

Tzintzuntzan is a land-poor community. In contrast to
nearby hamlets where many families own twenty to fifty
hectares, few Tzintzuntzeños own more than five hectares.
Moreover, the government-sponsored *ejido* program has not
been a local success because the lands assigned to Tzintzuntzan are located about five miles away. Only a dozen families
possess ejido lands and most exercise their rights through
sharecropping arrangements with farmers from other villages.
In the long run, this program seems to have had little impact
on the community.

FIG. 1-4—Roadside stands offer pottery and crafts to tourists (*above*); an arcade, built in 1974, also attracts tourists to buy local and regional folk arts (*below*).

Indirect Government Programs

We have discussed a number of government programs which have impinged directly on Tzintzuntzan during the past three decades. Tzintzuntzeños also have been affected by governmental actions carried out in other places for other purposes. For example, decisions to begin and terminate the bracero program were not made with Tzintzuntzan in mind. Planners examined the impact of such programs on all the "Tzintzuntzans" of rural Mexico, not just this one. Thus, when the government began massive construction projects for the subway in Mexico City, people from the whole nation responded—and Tzintzuntzeños were no exception. And as the flow of information into Tzintzuntzan improves, more villagers likely will respond to government-created job opportunities, whether in the local setting, in Mexico City, or in the United States.

INTERNATIONAL DEVELOPMENT PROGRAMS

UNESCO's Fundamental Education Training Center for Latin America (CREFAL)—established in the early 1950s at Pátzcuaro—carried out a major community development program in Tzintzuntzan for several years, stressing home egg production, pottery improvements, weaving, and furniture manufacturing. Foster has discussed the history of this project, and its sparse results (1967:327-347). None of the projects survived, and in that sense the program must be considered a failure. In another sense, however, it was successful. International and Mexican Government interest in the village led people to see that they were capable of dealing with outsiders; many of today's leaders gained great self-confidence during the CREFAL period of activity. And students from Latin American countries living with village families aroused their curiosity about the outside world and stimulated their desire to be more like this world.

THE ROLE OF PRIVATE ENTERPRISE

While government programs improved Tzintzuntzan's infrastructure, private enterprise brought the villagers into the urban world of consumption. The products of a wide variety of businesses, including those of multinational corporations, are now available in Tzintzuntzan. Conversely, local entrepreneurs, especially pottery resellers, now sell locally-produced goods in Mexico City, Guadalajara, and the northern border cities. And although no direct industrial development has come to Tzintzuntzan, emigrants from the village have benefited from industrialization in other regions of the country.

Mass Communication and Advertising

Of the many outside enterprises influencing Tzintzuntzan, perhaps the most important are the urban-based mass media. The role of radio and television in bringing villagers news of the outside world has already been mentioned. In addition, Tzintzuntzan—and thousands of similar rural communities—has become a target for mass advertising campaigns, which change people's buying habits and consumption patterns and, in turn, may improve their health and living conditions.

The local reaction to these blandishments has meant that local stores have had to carry a much broader inventory than in earlier years. One small store, for example, stocks more than 400 items, representing everything from local agricultural produce to canned foods from the Mexican affiliates of American manufacturers like Del Monte, McCormick, and Nabisco. Nonetheless, Tzintzuntzan has no open-air marketplace nor any *supermercados* or chain stores. Local residents and peasants living in neighboring hamlets must, therefore, travel to Quiroga, Pátzcuaro, Morelia, or beyond to acquire products and capital goods unavailable in the village. And it seems unlikely that outside investors will provide capital to build such facilities because of the small local population base and the presence of established competitors in nearby towns.

While radio and television are principal sources of news and advertising, newspapers and magazines are much less important in Tzintzuntzan. Beginning about 1965 the daily *La Voz de Michoacán*, the main provincial newspaper in the state, was brought from Morelia to Tzintzuntzan. At the height of its popularity the newspaper was distributed to about thirty subscribers. With the proliferation of television, however, the number of subscribers dropped to seven, and the local agent abandoned the service. Now, no newspapers or magazines come regularly to the village. In fact, because of their reliance on mass media originating in the capital, Tzintzuntzeños probably know more about life in Mexico City, key actors on the national scene, and major international news than they know about events on the other side of their own state.

Transportation and Tourism

Transportation enterprises also have had a significant impact on the community. Hundreds of trucks, buses, and cars pass through town every day. Many of these stop in Tzintzuntzan to load and discharge cargo and passengers. Approximately twelve buses per hour stop during the day and perhaps half that many at night. Thus, villagers easily can travel to Morelia, Mexico City, or other cities to buy goods or sell their products, to visit friends and relatives, to plead their case before state or federal officials, to seek temporary or permanent employment, or to receive specialized medical treatment beyond that offered in the local clinic. Furthermore, a number of Tzintzuntzeños now receive deliveries of liquid propane gas for their stoves from a Morelia distributor, and a few families even order purified bottled water from Morelia.

Outside business investment has been conspicuously absent in improving Tzintzuntzan's share of the growing tourist market. The village lacks a hotel, a tourist-class restaurant, a gas station, and a service garage. It is unlikely that these necessary services will ever be available in Tzintzuntzan, since they exist in nearby Quiroga and Pátzcuaro.

On the other hand, outside businesses have stimulated pottery and handicraft production. Large orders (e.g., a thousand ashtrays) from hotels and restaurants in Mexico City have provided considerable impetus to local pottery-makers. Recognition of the artistic merits of the pottery of the village's finer craftsmen has also meant improved sales; in order to meet the increased demands for their ware, Tzintzuntzan potters have "rationalized," at least partially, the production process. Heretofore each family was traditionally an independent, vertically-integrated production unit; but in recent years a number of potters have tried to create a modified assembly line production system. They contract with other families for unfired "green" ware to be delivered in specific quantities on certain dates; then they do the art work and firing of the pottery. Finally, the pottery is sold to a reseller, to one of the many pottery stands or stores (now numbering about fifty) which deal directly with tourists passing through town, or to the outside enterprise which contracted for the order.

Consumer Credit and Indebtedness

In recent years, a number of Tzintzuntzan families have gone into debt to outside creditors to purchase expensive consumer goods, to improve their homes, to buy a truck or car, or to expand their business. This installment buying also is encouraged by the government, whose agencies also sell many products to villagers on credit. Although no villagers currently have credit cards, some emigrants do; and their ability to make large purchases on time is certain to impress the more affluent village families. In fact, one store specializing in reselling pottery and handicrafts to tourists became affiliated with the BANCOMER credit card system in late 1973. The net effect of increased credit buying and indebtedness to outside businesses is to draw Tzintzuntzeños even more irrevocably into the urban sphere. This suggests that a useful measure of urbanization for rural communities would be the amount of accumulated debt and the proportion of families with credit accounts in urban businesses.

THE IMPACT OF INDIVIDUALS

Having examined the effect of government programs and private enterprise on Tzintzuntzan, we turn now to the impact of individuals on the community. The persons who influence Tzintzuntzan's development include persons born there who have emigrated, as well as persons born elsewhere who pass through the village. Because documentation of the impact of individuals on the urbanization process is difficult, and because the role of individuals is rather informal and random in comparison with governmental and business activities, the following discussion is necessarily impressionistic.

Non-Tzintzuntzeños: Mexicans and Foreigners

Many Mexican citizens stop in Tzintzuntzan to climb the pyramids, to visit the church and convent, or to buy pottery and crafts at the roadside stands and stores. In addition, many non-villagers work in Tzintzuntzan or come to the village as representatives of various government agencies or private companies. These outsiders provide Tzintzuntzeños with clues to the latest urban life styles, and they also help the local economy by their activities. There is, however, a small group of outsiders who come to the village and whose influence upon it is primarily negative. In recent years, some 25 homes have been constructed on the lake shore at the northern end of Tzintzuntzan, which serve as weekend and vacation retreats for wealthy families from Morelia. These visitors have little contact with local residents, except for the few caretakers they have hired to guard their properties and except for the few occasions when they come into town to buy supplies they forgot to bring from Morelia. Their major impact has been to withdraw several hectares of good agricultural land from the limited local supply and to force up the price of other lake shore properties in anticipation of further purchases.

While Mexicans represent the majority of tourists who stop in Tzintzuntzan, a number of foreigners also pass through the community. Because nearly all of these foreigners are Americans, the following discussion is limited to them. One consequence of their visits to the village is an increased interest in learning English. This, in turn, has had the unintended consequence of raising the status of adolescents and young adults, since they are more familiar with basic business English than are their parents. Another important effect of American tourists is in broadening villagers' horizons. Every day numerous Americans, ranging from children to hippies to retired persons, stop in Tzintzuntzan to see the sights and to haggle over the price of pottery and other handicrafts. In a sense, the Americans who pass through the village bear a responsibility of which they are probably unaware; they represent "Los Estados Unidos," the mythical land of opportunity, and this is so particularly for American tourists of Mexican ancestry. American tourists also provide Tzintzuntzeños with increased pride in their community. They ask questions about the Tarascan kings, about the church and convent, about who makes the best pottery, and about the future of the village. Many tourists already know much about Tzintzuntzan and their knowledge about the village is at once startling and gratifying to Tzintzuntzeños.

Tzintzuntzeños: Returned Migrants
and Permanent Emigrants

Urbanization does not always depend on strangers. Tzintzuntzeños also are active participants in Mexican development through their travels, their contacts with outsiders, and their permanent settlement in a number of cities. When they return to the village they bring new ideas, new aspirations, and new consumer goods. While returned braceros were responsible for many innovations, more recently local pottery resellers have become the most important native agents of change. Their contact with people travelling through Tzintzuntzan and their own travels to distant cities have convinced them that Tzintzuntzan is no longer an isolated village but is, instead, part of modern Mexico.

The relative success of Tzintzuntzeño emigrants in Mexican (and American) cities has also been very important in the community's development. Emigrants provide those who stay behind with models of how to cope with urban life. When they return for brief visits, longer vacations, or even to live once again in Tzintzuntzan, the emigrants also provide images of the city to their fellow villagers.

Among the small number (probably less than 50 in the past 30 years) of emigrants who return to live in Tzintzuntzan, some have returned because they lost their jobs in the city. More frequently, however, migrants go back home for non-economic reasons. One man said that his children were always ill in the city (where he and his family had lived in a crowded *vecindad*), but now in the village the children were again healthy. Another family also returned because they wanted to provide their children more room to play than was available in Mexico City. A few emigrants have returned to

FIG. 1-5—This migrant family has returned to the village where they now make pottery and sell crafts.

care for elderly relatives left alone as the children grew up and left the village to seek their fortunes elsewhere.

Most of the emigrants, therefore, do not return as "failures" from the urban scene; they choose to return, they do not seek refuge. Some emigrants even are buying lots and building vacation homes in Tzintzuntzan. Still others talk of retiring back to the village where the cost of living seems to them to be less than in the metropolis. They hope that their pensions will buy more for them and their families, but this will be true only if they readjust their living standards to those of the village. In a sense, Tzintzuntzan emigrants moving back to the village from Mexico City face the same problems of adjustment that they once faced when going to the city. They must find housing, employment, education for their children, and meaningful social relationships. At the same time, they must avoid tearing apart the fabric of village life by being haughty, by displaying their disproportionate wealth, or by comparing Tzintzuntzan unfavorably with their former urban residence. So far, this has not been a problem; but as the number of returned emigrants grows, the potential for social conflict increases.

Even those emigrants who seldom, or never, visit Tzintzuntzan contribute to its modernization. First they send remittances to their relatives back home. Although it is difficult to assess the quantity and frequency of money and merchandise sent back to the village, it is likely that most emigrants do send remittances with some regularity. One man now living in Mexico City, where he works for the government as a computer systems coordinator, sends about 1,000 pesos ($80 US) to his parents each month. Other migrants send from a few pesos to several hundred pesos regularly. If we suppose that the typical migrant sends an average of 100 pesos per month in money or merchandise, the aggregate remittance of the emigrant population would be over one million pesos a year. Even if the total remittances were half this amount, Tzintzuntzan is still receiving an excellent "return" on its emigrant "investment."

Second, emigrants provide their fellow villagers with assistance in looking for jobs and housing in the city. These ties to "senior" migrants have been crucial in the initial urban experience for more than 90% of Tzintzuntzeños now living in Mexico City. New migrants enter the urban scene as "clients" to those who preceded them. As a result, complex social networks bridge the gap between Tzintzuntzan and the capital, transforming what once were individual migration itineraries into a continuing, and expanding, social process. The set of actors is constantly changing, with each new emigrant profiting from the experiences—pleasant and unpleasant—of relatives and friends with whom he comes in contact (Kemper 1974:84-85).

Third, emigrants are sources of valuable information about city life. They take villagers sightseeing, escort them to re-

FIG. 1-6—A village band performs during the festival of the village's patron saint.

ligious shrines, show them national treasures, and in general convince them that the city is not a strange and dangerous place. Emigrants also serve as intermediaries when villagers need assistance in dealing with businesses, government agencies, or with admissions into the university system. In fact, with the current demand for higher education outstripping the government's ability to provide facilities, migrants are crucial middlemen in getting Tzintzuntzan's young people into normal schools, preparatories, and universities. The figures on current enrollment of Tzintzuntzeños in higher education indicate that they are very successful in this enterprise.

Finally, when emigrants return for ritual occasions, they validate the importance of Tzintzuntzan in the eyes of those who stay behind. A number of migrant women still return home to have their babies. Young children are often brought back to the local parish church for their baptism or confirmation. And many persons return for a few days during Holy Week, Christmas, or during the village fiesta in honor of *Nuestro Señor del Rescate*, held in the first part of February each year. In fact, when an "Agrupación de Tzintzuntzeños radicados fuera de su pueblo" was established in 1975, one of its primary functions was to venerate the local patron saint.

SUMMARY

The view from Tzintzuntzan suggests that its population is becoming increasingly active in Mexico's expanding urban system. The transformation of Tzintzuntzan, through the efforts of government, private enterprise, and certain individuals, has likely occurred in hundreds of similar communities. While modernization has had both positive and negative effects on Tzintzuntzan, its overall consequences have been beneficial to the community's inhabitants and to the progress of the nation.

CHAPTER 2

EMIGRATION FROM TZINTZUNTZAN

Tzintzuntzan peasants respond in several ways to the rapidly changing conditions in their community: some cling to increasingly out-dated traditions; others deviate from accepted norms of behavior in order to better their economic position within the community; and still others seek new opportunities by choosing to emigrate.

Like other Mexican peasants, many Tzintzuntzeños have traditionally travelled widely, especially in visiting distant religious shrines and in trading pottery and crafts for cheeses, dried meats, and fruits in the *tierra caliente*. By 1945—when the village population was 1,231—only 34 adults had not travelled beyond the local community, and 195 had been as far as Mexico City at least once (Foster and Ospina 1948:148). Today, Tzintzuntzan's location astride the Pátzcuaro-to-Quiroga highway results in excellent and frequent bus service, with connections at Quiroga to Mexico City, Guadalajara, and other destinations. A trip to Mexico City, for example, takes only about seven hours.

Where does the highway take emigrants from Tzintzuntzan? Analysis of ethnographic census data for the past 30 years shows that 41.0% of those who emigrate remain within the limits of Michoacán, 33.7% go to Mexico City, 5.8% go to the "Core Region," 4.7% go to the North, 2.5% go to the West, 0.2% go to the South, and 8.2% cross the frontier to settle in the United States. In addition, the destinations of 3.9% of the emigrants are unknown (Table 2-1 and Fig. 2-2). Although a plurality of the emigrants have remained in Michoacán, this is a "multiple" destination which includes the cities of Morelia, Pátzcuaro, and Uruapan, as well as a number of rural settlements. In contrast, Mexico City alone has received 303 emigrants, in spite of its greater

FIG. 2-1—The main highway through Tzintzuntzan. The bus stops for passengers at the plaza.

distance. The only cities other than Mexico City or those in Michoacán to receive appreciable numbers of emigrants are Tijuana, Guadalajara, and Toluca.

Of known emigration, 22.8% occurred since 1970, 54.7% between 1960 and 1969, 20.3% between 1945 and 1959, and only 2.2% prior to 1945.[1] In recent years Mexico City has become the predominant destination while migration within the state of Michoacán has diminished. Before 1960, only one of every sixteen village households had an emigrant member in Mexico City; between 1960 and 1970, about one in four households sent a member to the capital; today, probably one in three households has a direct tie to Mexico City through an emigrant member. The Core Region no longer attracts many migrants, because many of them continue on to Mexico City. In contrast, during the 1960s and the 1970s

TABLE 2-1
Regions of Destination

Period of Migration

Region[a]	Pre-1945	1945-1959	1960-1969	1970-1974[b]	Totals	%
Michoacán	9	89	212	59	369	41.0
Mexico City	10	50	186	57	303	33.7
U.S.A.	1	6	36	31	74	8.2
Core Region	0	29	11	12	52	5.8
North Region	0	8	18	16	42	4.7
West Region	0	0	17	6	23	2.5
South Region	0	0	2	0	2	0.2
Unknown	0	1	10	24	35	3.9
Totals	20	183	492	205	900	100.0
%	2.2	20.3	54.7	22.8	100.0	

[a]The Core Region consists of Aguascalientes, Guanajuato, Hidalgo, México, Morelos, Puebla, Querétaro, San Luis Potosí, Tlaxcala, and Veracruz. The West consists of Jalisco, Colima, Zacatecas, and Nayarít. The North consists of Baja California, Chihuahua, Coahuila, Durango, Nuevo León, Sinoloa, Sonora, and Tamulipas. The South consists of Campeche, Chiapas, Guerrero, Oaxaca, Tabasco, Yucatán, and Quintana Roo (cf. Cline 1963:49).

[b]Figures for 1970-1974 are estimates derived from interviews with selected key informants. All other figures are based on analysis of Foster's unpublished household census data for 1945, 1960, and 1970. Tables 2-2 through 2-5 are based on these same sources.

emigration to the north (mainly to border cities like Tijuana and Nogales) has become more frequent as a result of knowledge that ex-*braceros* acquired in their journeys. Moreover, nearly every Tzintzuntzan man possessing a valid work permit or passport now works across the border. Most of these men keep their families in Tzintzuntzan, but as finances permit they are arranging for their wives and children to join them in the United States or in the border area.

Internal migration was relatively more important for national population redistribution during the great industrial

FIG. 2-2—Destination regions for Tzintzuntzan emigrants.

expansion of the 1940s and 1950s than in the 1960s
(C.E.E.D. 1970:91). Thus, the temporal distribution of migration is not typical of Mexican national norms, since most
of its emigration has occurred since 1960. Apparently, the
bracero program effectively drained off many potential Tzintzuntzan emigrants, who reaped its temporary benefits while
retaining their community affiliations. With cancellation of
the program in 1964, this avenue to wealth through remittances was closed, and emigration to urban centers dramatically increased. As one Tzintzuntzan peasant remarked, "We
can see our *pueblo* growing smaller, especially because all the
young people leave home. They all go off to seek their fortune in Mexico City where they hope to find a job through
the aid of Tzintzuntzeños already there." While he overstates
the facts in two respects (the village population continues to

grow in absolute numbers, although the growth rate during the 1960s slowed markedly, from 3.5% to about 2% per annum, and only one-third of all emigrants go to Mexico City), he is correct that those who migrate usually are able to find steady employment and make significant progress by local standards.

During the past quarter century rural-*rural* (as contrasted to rural-*urban*) migration from Tzintzuntzan has been no more than one-fourth of all emigration (Table 2-2). In contrast to rural-urban migration, the traditional pattern of rural-rural migration from Tzintzuntzan primarily involves adjacent hamlets in the lake region and is primarily the consequence of marriage outside the village. The short distances, seldom more than a few hours' walk or canoe ride, do not inhibit frequent contacts and maintenance of strong personal ties with the long-time friends, neighbors, and relatives of many Tzintzuntzeños. The local church also plays an important role in continuance of close connections with Tzintzuntzan, since its parish includes the many nearby hamlets. Their inhabitants come to Mass each Saturday evening or Sunday morning, bring their children for baptism and first communion, and share in the yearly cycle of fiestas and religious rituals in Tzintzuntzan.

To what degree does rural-*urban* migration from Tzintzuntzan proceed by stages, that is, from village to small

TABLE 2-2
Rural-Urban Migration

Period of Migration

Destination	Pre-1945	1945-1959	1960-1969	1970-1974	Totals	%
Rural	1	53	94	41	189	21.0
Urban	18	126	354	140	638	70.9
Unknown	1	4	44	24	73	8.1
Totals	20	183	492	205	900	100.0

town to large city? First proposed for nineteenth-century England by Ravenstein (1885:198-199) and corroborated in large measure for the United States (e.g., Taeuber, Chiazze, and Haenzel 1968:95), the "stage migration" model has been widely reported for Latin America (Mangin 1967:79; Butterworth 1971:96; Herrick 1965:55; Germani 1961:212), but its applicability to Mexico has been questioned by several investigators.

For example, in his study of the Mixteca Alta village of Tilantongo, Butterworth reported that "Although some of the earlier migrants went first to smaller cities, such as Oaxaca, Veracruz, and Puebla, as indeed some still do today, the general pattern has not been one of stepwise migration from village to small city to capital city. . .Today the majority of migrants from Tilantongo go directly from their community to Mexico City" (1962:261). Similarly, in their study of migrants to Monterrey, Browning and Feindt found that, "Approximately one-half of all migrants had no conformity, complete or partial, to the stage migration model" (1971:321), partly because of the insufficiently developed urban hierarchy of regional towns in Mexico and partly because of transportation networks and utilization of available kinship affiliations. The evidence for Tzintzuntzan rural-urban migrants supports their conclusions. The earliest migrants often journeyed to Mexico City by stages, whereas nearly all recent migrants go directly.

Case histories will perhaps be more revealing here than further discussion of theoretical possibilities. The first two case histories reflect experiences of some of the earlier migrants; the next two involve villagers who have recently travelled to Mexico City.

RODOLFO CAMPOS: ENTREPRENEUR

After the death of his sole surviving parent, Rodolfo was sent to live in Pátzcuaro in 1935, at age 13, when no relative in Tzintzuntzan was able or willing to take him in. For six years he lived with his uncle's family, where he learned the tailor's trade. Then he joined his half-brother in Mexico City where, initially unable to find work, he considered returning to Pátzcuaro. Fortunately, however, he found part-time work as a tailor's helper and after a year became a telegraph messenger in the same office where his half-brother was employed. He married the younger sister of the woman who had married his half-brother and soon after moved onto a small lot on the northeastern periphery of the capital. He worked hard as a telegraph messenger and at other part-time jobs but for years made little economic progress. He earned enough to keep his three children in school through the secondary and vocational levels and to slowly improve the family's modest home. By 1976, some 35 years after coming to the capital, Rodolfo looks forward to retiring from the telegraph service and to working full time in the small liquor/grocery store he aquired in 1973. The profits from this enterprise have provided funds for building a second level on the house, where the oldest son, his wife, and child now live. In 1974, the family opened a small school supplies store across the street from a large school complex in an adjacent neighborhood. In 1976, they opened a small auto parts and service store next door to the school supplies store. Thus, at this time, Rodolfo owns three stores and is enjoying considerable entrepreneurial success. These are family firms in the truest sense: Rodolfo and a nephew run the liquor store; the eldest son, his wife, and sister run the school supplies store; and the remaining son and another nephew run the auto parts and service store. The recent success of these family enterprises promises to provide a much better foundation for the children's socioeconomic mobility than was true for Rodolfo, one of Tzintzuntzan's "pioneer" migrants to Mexico City.

JOSE ZAVALA: SCHOOL PRINCIPAL

Unable to finish primary school in Tzintzuntzan because of the church-state conflicts of the 1930s, José convinced his reluctant parents to send him to Morelia, where he completed sixth grade and later earned a teacher's credential. One of his teachers found a job for José in

Torreón, Coahuila, where he stayed from 1947 to 1952, until the same friend arranged a transfer for him to Mexico City. By that time, José had married a woman from Tzintzuntzan whose first husband had died and left her with two small children. After arriving in the capital, José and his wife had two more children. The family eventually was able to move into a government-subsidized housing project where they obtained a two-bedroom apartment. In addition to his own family, José arranged to take care of two nephews who came to Mexico City to pursue their higher education. By 1970, José had become a primary school principal through his own evening college studies. In 1973, the family moved to a house which they had had constructed on a lot near the airport, a few miles from the housing project. They left the apartment in the hands of their eldest son (who works as an art teacher), his wife, and baby. In 1975 José began to put into practice his ideas for a voluntary association of Tzintzuntzan migrants, and he continues to be the leader of this informal group. He is nearing retirement age and talks of moving back to the village where he and his wife have a house and still retain many family ties.

LEONARDO ZAMUDIO: FACTORY LABORER

Twenty-three year old Leonardo arrived in Mexico City in 1964, invited by an uncle with whom he stayed as a guest for more than a year. Although he did not find work immediately, he eventually became a laborer in an aluminum construction firm, where he worked for a year. Then he got a better-paying job with a rival firm, where he remained until 1972 when he shifted to the company where he still works as a "tenured" mechanic's helper earning the minimum wage. After his first job, Leonardo got an apartment with two other fellow migrants. Then he married a woman from Durango whom he had met in the neighborhood; they rented a room in an adjacent *vecindad* in the same far western peripheral zone and remained there for five years. Then they and their children moved to the city's northern periphery to caretake another migrant's home for a year. Subsequently, in 1975, they moved nearby into another one-room vecindad apartment. During his decade in the capital Leonardo has made little economic progress;

instead, it has been a constant struggle to survive on minimum wages plus overtime pay as his family has grown to six children.

EMILIANO GUZMAN: FACTORY WORKER

Emiliano first left Tzintzuntzan as a nineteen-year-old agricultural laborer. He went with an older brother to Texas in 1960 and then returned to the United States in 1964. He married a village girl in 1965 and lived in his parent's house until 1967, when he first travelled to Mexico City to seek work. He left his wife and baby in Tzintzuntzan and lived in the capital with her older brother. He soon found work and brought his wife and child to live with him in the same vecindad. His first job came through the aid of a friend he had first met while working as a bracero in Texas. He subsequently obtained two other jobs through friends, the first through a fellow migrant and the second from a union official. The birth of three more children forced a move to a larger vecindad and has caused Emiliano to buy a lot on the far western outskirts of the city where he is currently building his own house next to that of his in-laws. In sum, although Emiliano has a "tenured" job and earns above the minimum wage, he struggles to care for his four children, his wife, and a nephew who lives with them. He is optimistic about the future now that he has his own house and lot; the years in the vecindad, even in the company of friends and relatives, were difficult.

Although these four case histories represent only a small segment of the migrants, they illustrate the wide range of experiences, skills, and backgrounds present among the Tzintzuntzeños in Mexico City. In every case, the assistance of friends and relatives has been important to the success achieved by these individuals and their families. I shall give considerable attention to this point in subsequent discussions of social and economic mobility in the urban setting.

AGE AND SEX DISTRIBUTION OF MIGRANTS

At the time of their initial departure from the village, the great majority of Tzintzuntzeño emigrants are below age 30—with 31.5% between 0 and 15, 52.3% between 16 and 30, and only 16.2% over 30 (Table 2-3). The increase in the 0-15 age group for the period since 1960 is due to the exodus of whole families stimulated to emigrate because of increased competition for limited local resources within the traditional occupational categories of pottery-making and agriculture. In addition, the newly-affluent families of Tzintzuntzan are using wealth gained from storekeeping, pottery wholesaling, and sales to tourists at the *puestos* to send their older children away to secondary and vocational schools.

Tzintzuntzan differs from the national pattern with respect to male-female ratios in Mexican internal migration. Whereas for the country at large 100 females migrated for every 83 males (C.E.E.D. 1970:105) during the 1950s, in Tzintzuntzan there is a long-term trend toward equilibrium (Table 2-4). Unlike most villages in rural Mexico, Tzintzuntzan does not depend primarily on agricultural production for its livelihood; instead, pottery-making is the occupation of half the village households, and only a very few families own agricultural plots sufficient to their needs. As a result, young men who in many peasant villages would

TABLE 2-3
Age Cohorts of Migrants

Age Cohort at time of Emigration	Pre-1945	1945-1959	1960-1969	1970-1974	Totals	%
0-15	3	51	169	60	283	31.5
16-30	15	97	244	115	471	52.3
Over 30	2	35	79	30	146	16.2
Totals	20	183	492	205	900	100.0

TABLE 2-4
Sex of Migrants

Sex	Pre-1945	1945-1959	1960-1969	1970-1974	Totals	%
Male	10	84	252	114	460	51.1
Female	10	99	240	91	440	48.9
Totals	20	183	492	205	900	100.0

be occupied in their family *milpas* or hired out as *jornaleros* are limited to craft production in Tzintzuntzan. Since for many this is a poor source of income, they are stimulated to emigrate. In contrast, whereas young women in many villages often go to the cities to work as maids, in Tzintzuntzan young women may be skillful and productive potters who serve as important economic additions to their households. Consequently, they tend to remain at home. When this divergence from the usual occupational structure of Mexican peasant villages is combined with the long-term numerical superiority of live female births in Tzintzuntzan (107.5 to 100, according to Foster 1967:226), a situation of sexual equilibrium in emigration results.

Examination of migrant age group distribution reveals that men are slightly more numerous in the prime working years, whereas women are more numerous in both the youngest and oldest cohorts (Table 2-5). Since the differences in the 0-15 age group correspond almost exactly to the ratio of female-to-male live births in the village, we may conclude that the children of migrants are present in the expected ratio. In other words, sex selectivity does not operate among children but only for those persons (i.e., adults) actually making their own migration decision. The greater number of women in the "over 30" cohort is a result of their numerical predominance in the "widowed" and "separated" categories. These women often take their children with them when they seek a new life outside Tzintzuntzan, which in turn inflates the number of persons listed in the 0-15 age group.

TABLE 2-5
Age Cohorts and Sex of Migrants

Sex	0-15	16-30	Over 30	Totals
Male	135	255	70	460
Female	148	216	76	440
Totals	283	471	146	900

Analysis of the relevant age cohorts shows that the proportion of Tzintzuntzeños between 0-15 in 1945 was 16.2% (6.7% males and 9.5% females). By 1970, this same set of persons, represented by the 26-30 age cohort, totalled only 5.9% (2.6% males and 3.3% females) of the village population. This decline cannot be accounted for except through emigration. Similar declines can be observed through cohort analysis of Table 1-1 in the previous chapter. The 6-10 age cohort of 1945 had 14.0% of the village population; in 1970, as the 31-35 age cohort, it contained only 4.5% of the total. Even for the 1960-1970 period, substantial declines due to emigration are evident. Persons in the 6-10 age cohort in 1960 represented 16.0% of the village population; by 1970, as the 16-20 age cohort, they were only 10.4% of the total. Similarly, the 11-15 age cohort of 1960 was 12.5% of the total population; the 21-25 age cohort in 1970 represented just 6.6% of Tzintzuntzan's population.

MIGRANT SELECTIVITY

It should be clear from the preceding demographic data that the migrants are a "select" group; that is, they do not represent a random sample of the village population. This selectivity also operates in other dimensions, particularly with respect to the socioeconomic and psychological traits of migrants. In the following pages, we shall examine briefly several indicators (education, occupation, living standards, and innovativeness) for which data on migrants and non-migrants are available. Since the comparison requires a common baseline, I shall use the 1970 ethnographic census data for Tzintzuntzan to determine whether the migrants or non-migrants have superior characteristics on these indicators.[2]

EDUCATION

Tzintzuntzeños who emigrated prior to 1960 came from homes with somewhat higher than average levels of literacy,[3] but in recent years differences between migrant and non-migrant households have disappeared as educational aspirations permeate the entire community and as the number of migrants has increased. Early migrants had better educational preparation than did non-migrants, but since 1960 improvement in non-migrant educational levels has somewhat narrowed the gap. Nevertheless, migrants from Tzintzuntzan continue to be positively selected on the basis of educational achievement (Table 2-6).

OCCUPATION

Occupational selectivity implies that migrants come from households in which "higher" occupational levels exist than among non-migrant households. On the basis of a series of non-occupational factors (literacy, schooling, voting, living standard, and travel) applied to the several major occupational specialties in Tzintzuntzan, Foster (1967:297) ranks local occupations in descending order from merchants,

FIG. 2-3—Graduation ceremonies at the local primary school.

farmers, day laborers, fishermen, to potters. While pottery-making households do contribute numerically the most people to the emigrant group, a comparison of migrant and non-migrant pottery-making households indicates that neither potters nor their children emigrate in the expected proportion. For example, only 5 (of 165) potters' households had emigrants before 1960, and only 27 (of 170) had emigrants between 1960 and 1970. Both proportions are less than the average of 6% and 24% of all village households affected by migration to Mexico City for the respective periods. In contrast, nearly every other occupational category has had proportionately more migrants than their proportion of local economic activity would lead us to predict. Merchants (especially pottery resellers), day laborers, and farmers have been particularly important contributors to the migration stream. Thus, occupational selectivity operates positively

TABLE 2-6
Overall Educational Level in Tzintzuntzan

Before 1960

Category	Migrants		Non-Migrants	
	N	%	N	%
(0) Incomplete Primary	9	47.5	247	82.3
(1) Complete Primary	8	42.0	50	16.7
(2) Complete Secondary	2	10.6	0	0.0
(3) Complete Preparatory	0	0.0	1	0.3
(4) College +	0	0.0	2	0.7
Totals	19	100.0	300	100.0
Means	.634		.203	

1960-1970

Category	Migrants		Non-Migrants	
	N	%	N	%
(0) Incomplete Primary	34	47.1	179	59.7
(1) Complete Primary	22	30.6	87	29.0
(2) Complete Secondary	12	16.7	21	7.0
(3) Complete Preparatory	4	5.6	9	3.0
(4) College +	0	0.0	4	1.3
Totals	72	100.0	300	100.0
Means	.806		.577	

Source: Data derived from information in Foster's 1945, 1960, and 1970 censuses.

on Tzintzuntzan households to send out villagers best equipped to cope with urban occupational requirements, while also keeping relatively more potters—the least skilled by urban standards—in the home community.

LIVING STANDARDS

Just as Tzintzuntzeños who emigrate are most likely to come from homes with better-than-average educational levels and "higher" occupational levels, they also come from homes with above-average living standards. On the basis of our 30-point Standard of Living Index, households from which migrants came prior to 1960 had a higher mean score than non-migrant households (11.0 to 8.33), and recent improvements in non-migrant households failed to entirely close the gap between 1960 and 1970 (11.72 to 10.39). During the period of "pioneer" migration, only the "wealthiest" homes contributed more than their proportionate share to the migration stream, and since 1960—the "mass" migration phase—only the "wealthy" and middle-range homes have had more than their proportionate share of migrants. Specifically, of the 19 pre-1960 migrant households, 23% had Index scores of 13 to 17 and 27% had scores of 18 or higher, whereas of the 300 non-migrant households for the same period, just 24% had scores of 13 to 17, and just 3% had scores of 18 or higher.

For the 1960-1970 period, the results are closer but still show a disparity between migrant and non-migrant households: of the 72 migrant households, 32% had scores of 13 to 17 and 17% had scores of 18 or higher; of the 300 non-migrant households, 24% had scores of 13 to 17 and 12% had scores of 18 or higher. In neither period did the "poor" households approach the number of migrants which their proportion in the community would lead us to predict. However, as the overall living standards in Tzintzuntzan have improved and the number of migrants has increased during the 1960s and 1970s, a clear "regression toward the mean" (Browning and Feindt 1969:356) has occurred for migrants to Mexico City.[4]

This finding reinforces the common observation that under really desperate conditions very few persons will risk emigration, whereas when wealth increases and is more widely distributed and when living conditions improve, the number of migrants increases and the degree of positive selectivity declines proportionately. One consequence of this trend is that more recent migrants, some of whom are likely to be less prepared to cope with urban life, may encounter greater difficulties than did earlier migrants in establishing themselves in Mexico City.

INNOVATIVENESS

If socioeconomic indicators alone explained migrant selectivity, then all households with high levels of education, occupation, and living standards would have sent migrants to Mexico City. Since this is not so, additional factors must operate in determining who goes and who stays at home. Browning (1971:167) has suggested that a "propensity for risk-taking" is an important characteristic of migrants which differentiates between those who actually leave and those who are content with their lot in the village. If this is true, then we can speculate that Tzintzuntzan migrants to Mexico City are more adventurous, more restless, and more ambitious than their counterparts who remain at home. Although this may appear to be an obvious fact, it is crucial to the eventual success of Tzintzuntzeños in the urban sector—for if those who migrate are at once best equipped on socioeconomic bases and by their psychological propensity to accept and overcome risks, then their chances of succeeding are much higher than would be the chances for persons with different characteristics.

Since we have no data on "risk-taking propensity" per se for Tzintzuntzan, I have analyzed Foster's empirically derived list of "innovators" in order to measure this psychological indicator.[5] Among the 68 households identified as containing at least one innovator—52 (76%) have had some member emigrate, and of these 23 have gone to Mexico City. Thus, we find that among non-migrant households only 15% contain innovators, whereas among migrant households approximately 25% are innovators. Although this somewhat simple measure of psychological selectivity of migrants to Mexico City is not differentiable according to pre- and post-1960 periods partly because certain individuals continue to innovate and partly because innovation tends to run in particular families, I believe that the declining selectivity found on all three socioeconomic indicators also exists for innovativeness.

Nevertheless, tendency to innovate and propensity to assume risks appear as important components of Tzintzuntzan migrants in comparison with non-migrant villagers. To paraphrase Butterworth (1969:342)—the meek, the less ambitious and adventurous, the rigid traditionalists are the people who stay in Tzintzuntzan. Those who have travelled to other cities and regions, who have talked with visitors and tourists, who are basically curious, flexible, willing to take risks, and achievement-motivated are the prime candidates for migration to Mexico City.

MIGRATION AND WORLDVIEW

Traditional Tzintzuntzan attitudes proscribed the emigration of certain persons, such as unattached young women, while forcing out others, especially those who commit crimes such as robbery or murder. Although Tzintzuntzan is a peaceful community in comparison to some Mexican villages, during the past three decades at least thirteen men, most of them with families, have fled to avoid the vengeance of a victim's relatives. "Forced" emigration probably constitutes about 10% of all population exodus from Tzintzuntzan and therefore must be considered an important "push" from communities where no other alternative from certain reprisal is available.

Of course, nearly all emigrants leave Tzintzuntzan of their own volition in response to their perception of local conditions vs. outside opportunities. Lack of fulfilling work and dissatisfaction with local economic prospects often provides an initial incentive to emigrate. The decision to leave the village also reflects a perception of what constitutes the "good life" and what are the possibilities for achieving it in Tzintzuntzan as compared with another community. Tzintzuntzeños weigh many features of village life when they decide to migrate; but the need to enjoy better living conditions and to get a superior education are sufficiently strong to override concerns about the hectic lifestyle, overcrowded living conditions, and exposure to unknown perils in their places of destination.

The attitudes of Tzuntzuntzeños toward traditional life and toward emigration were manifest in their stories narrated in response to Murray's Thematic Apperception Test (TAT)[6]. The stories cover a wide range of situations in which the predominant emotions, sentiments, personality conflicts, and anxieties can be expressed. The TAT was administered to a representative sample of Tzintzuntzeños in the capital; and on the whole, their responses were free and spontaneous.[7]

Although the TAT pictures are intentionally ambiguous, so as to stimulate the respondents' imagination and creative powers, many narratives dealt with themes related to migration. The following two stories illustrate typical migrant attitudes toward emigration:

CARD 13B—A little boy is sitting on the doorstep of a log cabin.

NARRATOR—26-year-old bachelor

A boy of very humble birth grew up in the countryside. He didn't know about a very different aspect of life: life in the city. One time, his parents took him to the capital, and he was surprised by the active way of life there: he saw new things, saw children of his age who were totally different in looks, in clothing, and in happiness all coming from living in the city where modern comforts are available. This remained etched in his mind. Upon returning to the countryside, he spent his days thinking about how he might come to live like those children he had seen in the city; but around him he saw only animals, plants, and poverty—and time passed without his achieving his desires. So, he demanded that his parents let him go live in the city. Finally, after a long period of poverty, he got his wish. He didn't achieve it at the age of the children he had met, but later on, in his adolescence, in his adulthood. He was happy, dressed well, and enjoyed his work. He managed to become someone who didn't lack all the necessary things of modern life. And above all, in the city he began to improve and develop himself.

CARD 2—In the foreground is a young woman with books in her hand; in the background a man is working in the fields and an older woman is looking on (country scene).

NARRATOR—17-year-old single girl

This is the story of a country girl who lived on a *rancho*. From childhood she had aspirations to become a great teacher. She grew up studying the primary grades in the village and had aspirations to be successful. Her parents were worried because they couldn't offer her what she desired. The girl helped in the household chores, but always with a book in her hand. She wished to learn more than she already knew. Finally, she came to the capital to study and to work, in order to achieve her childhood dreams. She realized her amibitions, became a teacher, and sent money back to her parents, so that they might also be able to progress. She was a great teacher and continued to strive after knowledge just as she always had done.

Migration to the capital is thus seen as a means of self-improvement and achieving one's aspirations. Migration is not a selfish move, however; children recall the sacrifices of their families and intend to repay suffering and poverty by assisting their siblings to progress and by helping their parents lead a better life in the village. Thus, achievement motivation is closely related to a preoccupation for nurture among the migrants. Unlike most peasants in Tzintzuntzan and similar communities, the migrants do not see suffering as a passive way of life by which one manipulates others (cf. Nelson 1971:114); in contrast, for Tzintzuntzeños who go to Mexico City self-sacrifice leads to the attainment of internalized aspirations and to a strong achievement orientation. Nurture, then, does not appear to express a concern for inadequacy and independence among Tzintzuntzan migrants but implies a strong sense of self-control and an orientation to attaining future goals through which one can make the balance with previous sacrifices by one's parents. The following two narratives illustrate the positive relationship between achievement and nurture for Tzintzuntzan migrants.

CARD 2—Country scene.

NARRATOR—Married woman, age 36

I think this is a family: those are the mother and father, and this must be the daughter. As they are *campesinos* ("peasants"), the girl has been growing up in the countryside. Now, being older, she is interested in her education (as we see from her books), wants to improve her life, and grow up to be a professional woman—so that she can escape the situation in which her parents live. According to what I see, she wants to progress in life and once she has grown up and has a career and lives a little better off, she perhaps can help her parents.

CARD 13B—A little boy is sitting on the doorstep of a log cabin.

NARRATOR—Bachelor, age 20

I see a boy at the door of a very poor house. He is thinking that his family has always suffered in poverty and thinks about escaping from his situation. He thinks about studying, working, and making a lot of money to improve his economic conditions. In the future he will live someplace else where he will be better off socially, will have a well-paying job, and be able to help his parents. He is preoccupied about this problem and searches for its solution. Then, he finds the answer: he will devote all his time to working to get out of his present poverty, to helping his parents and siblings—to helping his family. He will accomplish all this by getting a good job and making good money and without having problems in the near future.

SUMMARY

In conclusion, it should be clear that to date the bulk of Tzintzuntzan emigrants have been well prepared to cope with life outside the village. They are positively selected according to criteria such as education, occupation, living standards, and innovativeness. Their demographic characteristics also make them excellent candidates for succeeding in the urban arena of social and economic competition. Indeed, the transformation of Tzintzuntzan through its involvement with outside forces is mirrored by the increase in emigration to all areas of Mexico (and the United States, as well), especially Mexico City. The impact of emigration of Tzintzuntzan has so far been quite favorable and widespread. It remains to be seen what the effect of the apparent decline in "selectivity" will mean to the success of migrants in urban centers. Of course, it may be that the continuing improvement in most villagers' circumstances will permit nearly all emigrants to carry the credentials that once were borne only by the elite "pioneers."

Notes for Chapter Two

1. Since no accurate record of emigration from Tzintzuntzan is available for the period before the 1945 census, the figures for "before 1945" are based only upon known cases of emigration from the village. There appears to have been little migration beyond the immediate lake region before the mid-1930s. Nearly all migrants listed in the Tables as "before 1945" actually left Tzintzuntzan after the construction of the highway through the town in 1939.

2. Some important differences exist between the demographic selectivity of migrants to Mexico City and those to all other destinations. Tzintzuntzeños who have gone to Mexico City were slightly younger than those who went elsewhere; they included proportionately more males than did migrants to other places (sex ratio was 138/100 for the former, but reversed to 85/100 for the latter); and they included fewer widowed or separated persons. Thus, on demographic grounds at least, Tzintzuntzan migrants to the capital constitute a more "select" group than do Tzintzuntzeños who have gone elsewhere. Although I have not examined in detail the socioeconomic and psychological indicators of migrant selectivity for the households of Tzintzuntzan migrants to other destinations, I believe that they would be less selective than those whose members have gone to Mexico City, although probably more selective than households having no migrants at all. For the present analysis, households with migrants to destinations other than Mexico City were included in the non-migrant category and this did not distort the positive selectivity of the households whose members went to the capital.

3. Literacy levels in the pre-1960 period were 63.1% for heads of migrant households vs. 58.7% for non-migrant households. For the post-1960 period, the ratio shifted to 69.4% vs. 70.7%. In other words, although literacy of both migrant and non-migrant categories improved,

that of the latter group improved slightly more rapidly and thereby closed the previous gap.

4. On the basis of a similar analysis in the community of Tilantongo, Oaxaca, Butterworth (1969:316) came to very much the same conclusions: "Ordering migration data by wealth divisions reveals that a higher proportion of wealthier people have left Tilantongo for other areas of the Republic. . . .Furthermore, there are significantly different patterns of migration between the wealthy and the poor. Migration of the poor is usually seasonal and/or proximate. . . .Those in the middle and upper wealth categories were more likely to have gone to Puebla and Mexico City to work."

5. Foster defines innovation very broadly to cover the introduction of "anything new," such as "sending a child away to secondary or commercial school, acquiring a sewing machine, a radio, a steel plow, a truck, a nixtamal mill, using a chemical fertilizer, insecticides, hybrid seed, a toothbrush, renting a tractor or a threshing machine, developing new pottery techniques and styles, and many more" (1967:294-295). Since most of the items according to which "innovation" is measured also carry in their use a large degree of "risk-taking," it appears that the correlation between the two variables is sufficiently close to allow us to employ the list of innovators to measure the same sort of psychological selectivity that Browning's "propensity for risk-taking" would apply to.

6. Murray's Thematic Apperception Test, usually referred to as the TAT, is widely used as a psychological technique for revealing a subject's emotions, sentiments, and personality conflicts. The subject is shown a set of pictures, which in the present instance totalled 14 for females and 15 for males, and is asked to make up narratives about them in which he uses his imagination and creative abilities. The pictures are of varying degrees of ambiguity and may be interpreted in any way in which the subject chooses. In this way, psychologists infer from themes and principal concerns in the stories what are the values and preoccupations, the anxieties and fears, of the subject. In giving the TAT to Tzintzuntzan migrants, however, I have chosen to focus on the

cultural content of the stories rather than to attempt to analyze individual personalities. Thus, the TAT is used primarily to elucidate migrant perceptions of social roles and values, particularly as these relate to the conflict between tradition and modernism, between village and city, and between remaining in Tzintzuntzan and emigrating to Mexico City. The TAT has seldom been applied to the study of rural-urban migrants, but where it has been used it has proved to be a powerful supplementary tool to the traditional techniques of the ethnographer (e.g., Rotondo et al. 1963; De Ridder 1960).

7. The sample of Tzintzuntzan migrants consisted of 15 persons (10 males and 5 females) belonging to six different households in Mexico City. The sample was chosen to elicit differences based on socioeconomic status, length of urban residence, age and sex, and type and size of family.

CHAPTER 3

MEXICO CITY AS DESTINATION

Just as Tzintzuntzan was the capital of the Tarascan empire, so Mexico City (then known as Tenochtitlan) was the center of Aztec hegemony over much of Mesoamerica in the late pre-Conquest era. At its height, the island capital of Tenochtitlan was surely one of the largest and most splendid urban centers in the world. It was transformed by the Spanish into Mexico City and ever since has been the heart of Mexican politics, economics, and society.

Today, the urban area of metropolitan Mexico City has outstripped its city limits and those of the Federal District in which it is located. Indeed, most recent growth has taken place in the peripheral zones lying within the State of Mexico, which surrounds the Federal District on the west, north, and east. Between 1930 and 1970, Mexico City grew from 1.2 million to more than 8.5 million residents; and by 1975, it had added two million more people. Despite recent government appeals for decentralization, there is little hope that the metropolis will soon slow its rapid growth. One projection, by the United Nations, suggests that the metropolitan area of Mexico City will reach 32 million persons by the year 2000. In such circumstances, what continues to attract migrants to the capital? Why do Tzintzuntzeños and thousands of other Mexican villagers and city dwellers keep coming to an urban agglomeration with shortages of water, adequate housing, and municipal services? What makes the struggle for survival in Mexico City more easily endured than that in the migrant's home community?

In the preceding chapters we have examined some of the reasons why Tzintzuntzeños are stimulated to leave the village; here we turn to those characteristics of Mexico City which make it such an attractive urban destination. By comparing its demographic situation, economic structure, living standards, educational system, and communications networks with regional and national analogues, we can appreciate why so many Tzintzuntzan migrants choose the capital as the place in which to "search for life."

DEMOGRAPHIC SITUATION

Mexico City is without peer as the nation's primary urban center. It is six times larger than Guadalajara, the second largest city in the country, and has a metropolitan population greater than the next dozen cities in Mexico's urban hierarchy. Its share of the total national population has more than doubled, from 7.9% to 17.4%, in the period between 1940 and 1970; and its share of the nation's urban population has held steady at nearly 40% despite the rapid urban growth of intermediate size cities along the northern border (Table 3-1). The rapid growth of the capital is not due primarily to higher birth rates nor lower death rates than those of surrounding regions. On the contrary, the city population's fertility rate has been somewhat lower and the mortality index somewhat higher than national averages. It is the influx of cityward migrants which has brought the capital's population increase to the world's attention.

During the 1960-1970 period, for instance, migrants represented 37.5% of Mexico City's population growth. In this decade alone, 1.4 million persons came to the metropolitan area, and 58% of these came from states with high emigration rates such as Guanajuato, Hidalgo, Guerrero, Michoacán, Oaxaca, Puebla, and Veracruz (Corona Rentería 1974:296). Despite governmental efforts at decentralization, there is little hope that the tide of migrants can be slowed in the near future. In conjunction with the high rate of natural growth among both natives and migrants in the capital, continuing immigration to metropolitan Mexico City may boost the city's population to 15 million by 1980 and to 32 million by the end of the century, according to recent estimates by the United Nations.

Much of the metropolitan growth is by annexation of peripheral zones into the urban area (Table 3-2). Indeed, most of the actual growth is now concentrated in areas beyond the city limits proper and within the adjacent State of Mexico. The most spectacular case is the area known as Ciudad Netzahualcoyotl, an agglomeration of slums, squatter settlements, and subdivisions located on the dusty plains of long-dessicated Lake Texcoco east of the central city area. This suburban zone now has more than 800,000 persons (if not a million; population estimates for the area are notoriously low) and thus constitutes one of the largest urban *municipios* in the nation (Fig. 3-1).

ECONOMIC STRUCTURE

Despite the population problems outlined above, the rapid industralization of Mexico City to date has provided sufficient employment opportunities for semiskilled, skilled, and technical workers so that most natives and migrants have been able to find work. As Balán observes (1969:18-19), competition for jobs and better educational preparation of young people have in recent years required that more workers have basic "credentials" (i.e., primary school diploma) to obtain permanent employment. Today, a primary school diploma can provide union membership and a common laborer's job; within a decade the secondary school diploma may be necessary.

The changing pattern of employment tells us much about this rapid industrialization. In 1940, 62% of the city's "economically active population" was in the tertiary ("services") sector, 31.5% in the secondary ("industrial") sector, and just 7% in the primary ("agricultural/mining") sector. By 1960, although 58% was still in the tertiary sector, the secondary sector had increased to 39%, while the primary sector had declined to only 3%. In contrast, the national economy is still dominated by the primary sector: in 1960, 55% of the total

TABLE 3-1

Total Population and Urban Population of Mexico and
Population of the Mexico City Urban Area: 1930–1970

Population[1] Category	1930	1940	1950	1960	1970
(1) Total Population	16,553	19,649	25,779	34,923	49,100
(2) Urban Population	2,891	3,928	7,210	12,747	22,100
(3) Mexico City Urban Area Population	1,049	1,560	2,872	4,910	8,567
Percentages					
(4) (3)/(1) x 100	6.3	7.9	11.1	14.1	17.4
(5) (3)/(2) x 100	36.3	39.7	39.8	36.9	38.7

[1] Thousands of inhabitants.

Source: Adapted from C.E.E.D. 1970:118 (Table V-1) and Unikel 1971:510.

TABLE 3-2

Population[1] of Mexico City, the Federal District, and
the Mexico City Urban Area: 1930–1970

Territorial Unit	1930	1940	1950	1960	1970
(1) Mexico City	1,029	1,448	2,235	2,832	2,907
(2) Federal District	1,229	1,757	3,050	4,670	6,967
(3) Urban Area	1,049	1,560	2,872	4,910	8,567
(4) Urban Area in Federal District	1,049	1,560	2,861	4,677	6,855
(5) Urban Area in State of Mexico	–	–	11	233	1,712
Percentages					
(6) (1)/(3) x 100	98.0	92.9	77.8	57.7	33.9
(7) (4)/(3) x 100	100.0	100.0	99.6	95.3	80.0
(8) (5)/(3) x 100	0.0	0.0	0.4	4.7	20.0

[1] Thousands of inhabitants.   Source: Unikel 1971:510.

national manpower was devoted to agricultural pursuits, 18% to industry, and 27% to services.

With its huge share of national manpower, Mexico City increasingly controls equivalent shares of production and consumption: its metropolitan Gross Regional Product (GRP) represented 22% of the Gross National Product (GNP) in 1950; 30% in 1960, and 38% in 1970. On a per capita basis, its GRP expanded at an annual rate of 3.9% between 1950 and 1960, whereas the GNP grew only 2.6% per annum for the same period. Similarly, Mexico City absorbs about 35% of all merchandise produced in the nation, while the next largest urban centers—Guadalajara and Monterrey—consume only 6.4% and 4.7%, respectively (L.M.S. 1968:12-14).

Mexico City residents collect more than 30% of all wages and salaries paid to Mexican workers, and recent increases in the minimum wage levels may accentuate rural-urban and regional differentials (Table 3-3). In addition, the capital has a much larger middle and upper class than does Michoacán state or the nation at large. Furthermore, since the average income of *capitalinos* is about twice that of rural workers, this provides an attraction to the peasants of Tzintzuntzan and similar Mexican villages. But, even when compared with other large Mexican cities, the capital's economic structure still exercises a powerful "pull" on potential migrants.

STANDARD OF LIVING

Residents of Mexico City experience an exceedingly wide range of living conditions, but whatever their situation, it is almost always superior to that of the equivalent stratum of rural Mexican society. This relatively higher urban standard of living is due both to the proportionately higher incomes of the urban population and to government budgets which heavily subsidize basic urban services in Mexico City.

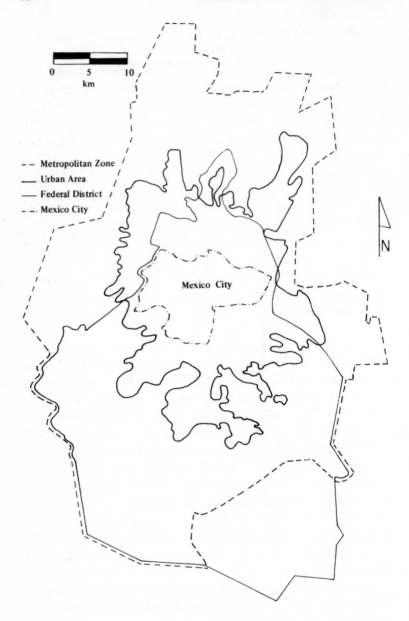

FIG. 3-1—The Mexico City metropolitan area and its subdivisions.

TABLE 3-3
Income Distribution[1]
Mexico City, Michoacán and the Nation–1970

Monthly Income Levels[2]	Nation	Michoacán	Mexico City
0– 199 pesos	16.50	21.75	3.49
200– 499 pesos	23.73	30.74	11.96
500– 999 pesos	24.14	20.42	30.25
1,000–1,499 pesos	11.35	5.01	22.14
1,500–2,499 pesos	7.32	2.96	14.77
2,500–4,999 pesos	4.28	1.79	9.24
5,000–9,999 pesos	1.54	0.64	3.63
10,000+	0.83	0.55	1.61
No Data	10.31	16.14	2.91
Totals	100.00	100.00	100.00

[1] In percentages. [2] Based on 1970 income levels.

Source: Censo General de Población (1970), Resumen General 1971:XXI, 117, 215.

Living standards are best understood by comparison with those of other regions and cities. Since researchers have not established a uniform "Standard of Living Index," we present data for a wide range of items which contribute to overall levels of living. First, to compare Mexico City with Michoacán, the home state of Tzintzuntzeños, in the context of national averages, illustrates the vast gap between conditions in a predominately rural region and in the capital: on nearly every indicator, Michoacán falls short of national norms, while Mexico City far surpasses them (Table 3-4). Second, to compare Mexico City with other large cities demonstrates that its living standards are higher than those in all major towns and cities except for Monterrey, the industrial giant of the north (cf. Unikel and Necochea 1971).

Thus, it is not surprising that Tzintzuntzan migrants to Mexico City experience a feeling of "relative affluence," no matter how poor their objective living conditions appear to an outside observer. Their standard of comparison is not

some mythical national norm but what they left behind in
Tzintzuntzan.

HOUSING

The rapid population growth and extensive industrialization of Mexico City has created a huge, unfulfilled demand
for adequate single-family and multi-family housing. Not
only is there a shortage of housing stock but perhaps half of
the units now inhabited are considered by local authorities to
be below minimum living standards. Housing in Mexico City
falls into several categories: (1) luxury homes located in a
few select neighborhoods in intermediate and suburban
zones; (2) well-constructed homes, condominia, and apartments for the upper-middle and middle classes found
throughout the metropolitan area but concentrated in plan-

TABLE 3-4
Standard of Living
in Mexico City, Michoacán, and the Nation—1970

Item	Mexico City[1]	Michoacán[2]	Nation[3]
	%	%	%
Electricity (home access)	94.84	50.16	59.51
Social Security Benefits[4] (1965)	34.60	5.20	16.00
Barefoot Population	0.55	3.00	6.88
Sandal/Shoe Wearers	0.36	18.40	13.15
Meat eaten every day	31.51	12.24	16.81
Sewage Disposal Access	77.52	32.47	41.12
Water: (home access or building)	81.77	39.11	49.13
Bathroom in home	57.69	20.89	31.47
Households with 3+ rooms	48.70	25.20	33.25
Gas/Electric Stoves	79.56	29.79	44.09
Radio/Television	69.50	16.77	30.62

Sources: [1]IX Censo General de Población (1970), Resumen General 1971:118,
    123-124, 126; [2]ibid.:216, 221-222, 224; [3]ibid.:XXII, XXVII-XXVIII, XXX;
    [4]data derived from Navarrete 1970:71, Table 8.

ned subdivisions; (3) moderately priced houses and apartment projects for the middle class constructed by the families themselves or built with government assistance and concentrated on the expanding peripheries; (4) low-quality houses and *vecindad* apartments for the working class spread throughout the metropolis; (5) peripheral *colonias proletarias* (squatter settlements and quasi-legal subdivisions); and (6) the *jacales* (shacks) found in small enclaves and in the *tugurios* and *ciudades perdidas* (slums).

Because the bulk of migrants reside, at least for a time if not permanently, in one or more types of lower-income and middle-income housing, it is appropriate to describe them in more detail. It is important to note that these housing types are often transitory. A neighborhood may begin as a series of wooden shacks and be transformed into an area of concrete block homes. Dirt paths become paved streets; electricity becomes available—clandestinely in the beginning and then through legal connections—to each dwelling; water and sewage service is provided; and, finally, schools and the full range of municipal services become available to an area once devoid of people or houses. Second, migrants as well as natives are highly mobile in their search for better housing at an affordable price. As we shall see in Chapter 4, people may move many times from the location of their first residence to the place where they manage to build their own home. The interaction of changing neighborhood facades and a mobile population provide a complex setting within which certain types of housing can be understood.

Tugurios and Ciudades Perdidas

Slums may consist of a few shacks or cover several blocks and contain hundreds of dwellings made of wood, cartón, or scrap sheets of tin. They appear to be chaotically arranged and to lack minimal urban services. No good contemporary estimates of the population of the slum zones are available, but it seems certain that at least one million people live in these substandard situations in more than 450 zones within the metropolitan area. A principal characteristic of these slums is their illegal or quasi-legal occupation of urban land. As Jackson (1973:30-31) has observed: "The center of an otherwise normal appearing city block may be filled with hundreds of shacks or. . .a railroad right-of-way may be expropriated with shacks extending almost to the tracks. Rooftop squatters may be yet another form of *ciudad* living. Tacit approval of the owner may be obtained, but 'rent' paid by the tenant will be in services. Ciudades located on the city's dumps allow the squatters space while the family works sorting the trash as it arrives."

Although the slums are notorious for harboring the poorest, most "marginal" elements of the urban population, both native and migrant, they do not provide an important niche for Tzintzuntzan peasants in Mexico City. Only one family resides in a wooden shack within a slum zone, and this instance appears to be due to the settlement's proximity to a factory where the household head works. Furthermore, there is little evidence to suggest that many Tzintzuntzeños have ever resided in the ciudades perdidas. The slums are a consequence of the exploding urban population of the recent decades; they grew up within traditional working class zones as a kind of internal marginal settlement. In recent years, this niche has tended to be filled by poor urban dwellers with some urban experiences, rather than by newly arrived migrants to the city. Thus, the slums appear to be less of a way-station on the path to the periphery than a dead end for those persons lacking the skills to succeed in the urban economic arena.

Vecindades

Multi-family dwellings, with shared toilets, common water taps, and cramped quarters, are the fate of many migrants

FIG. 3-2—Two brothers and their families rent rooms in this vecindad.

and natives in Mexico City. These vecindades are found throughout the city—from multi-storied, centrally located Spanish colonial buildings converted into a series of one-room apartments around a central patio to small, recently constructed multi-family buildings in the expanding peripheral zones. Although reliable estimates are lacking, it is probable that about 20% of all urban residents live in the rented rooms of vecindades. This mode of living provides a few more amenities that the ciudades perdidas, especially in terms of improved water and sanitary facilities. In contrast to the slums, the vecindades are usually recognized by the authorities as a regular and legal aspect of the housing stock of the metropolitan area.

Vecindad residents pay rents ranging from 100 to 300 pesos per month for their apartments, which usually have a single sleeping/living room about 10 x 10 ft plus a small kitchen area about 5 x 10 feet. The number of apartments may range from a low of five or six to a high of fifty or sixty.

In this context, the vecindad serves as a "little community" within which its residents have a ready reference group able to provide assistance in times of difficulty. For young migrant families the vecindad is a common residence type. It meets their limited need for space while providing them with social contacts which may open new opportunities for better housing and for better jobs. Vecindades are also obvious choices for migrants and natives who wish to live in extended family situations rather than in the isolation of nuclear family households. As we shall see in Chapter 5, for the Tzintzuntzan migrants the vecindad has become an important scene for their social adaptation to urban living patterns.

COLONIAS PROLETARIAS

Squatter settlements, quasi-legal subdivisions, and "regularized" neighborhoods compose a growing share of the urban area's housing stock. The traditional slums and vecindad zones are essentially filled to capacity. The colonias proletarias, on the other hand, are expanding in all directions as the city continues to attract new residents from other regions and as the natural population growth of the city itself spills over into surrounding zones. Each colonia probably has several thousand residents at minimum and contains a wide range of housing types—wooden shacks; vecindad multifamily units; and self-built, low income housing.

In recent years, it has become increasingly difficult to tell the illegal subdivisions from the legal settlements. The government has attempted to "regularize" residents' titles to land and homes, although this is a time-consuming, bribe-laden enterprise for too many residents. The provision of street lighting, water, sewers and drainage, paved streets, schools, medical clinics, and other environmental and social amenities is now fairly widespread in the colonias. For the three or four million people who see a peripheral neighborhood as a goal, because it will be the site of their own home, the colonias represent the final step in urban mobility. Nonetheless, it is clear that there exists considerable mobility within these zones, as residents go from one multi-family dwelling to another during the period when they try to save funds sufficient to qualify for a loan to buy a lot and build a house. The rapid and continuing growth of these neighborhoods is best seen in the Ciudad Netzahualcoyotl area, which contains at least sixty colonias. It is also visible in specific colonias carved out of the interstitial zones of the expanding urban area. One such colonia, Xalpa, is of particular interest because it became the home of some eleven Tzintzuntzan migrant families since the middle 1960s.

Xalpa is situated in the *delagación* of Atzcapotzalco northwest of the center of the city along the political boundary line which separates the Federal District from the State of Mexico. "Located on a rapidly disappearing garbage dump and surrounded by factories, it is a jumble of houses, shacks, and even some vecindades. Some of these dwellings are built on top of elevated piles of refuse, others in still to be filled depressions. Owners, renters, and squatters make up this most heterogeneous group" (Jackson 1973:34). What is at once so remarkable and typical is the colonia's rapid transformation in the past five years. Streets have been straightened and paved, street lighting is common, water and drainage is now available (except for periods of breakdown, during which people trek to the local pumping station to fill their water buckets). From my first visit to Xalpa in 1969 (when I trudged through muddy paths to visit a migrant family living in a shack next to a garbage dump) to my latest visit in 1976 (when I rode there on a first-class bus along well-paved streets), I have been impressed at the community's modernization. The garbage dumps have disappeared, their place taken by houses, stores, recreational fields, and schools. This same process is being repeated in hundreds of other neighborhoods throughout the metropolis.

Middle Income Housing

In contrast to the considerable social scientific and urban planning literature on low-income housing, relatively little is available on middle-income neighborhoods (and, of course, even less is known about upper-income areas). The economic progress of recent years has created a large market for good quality homes and condominium apartments in Mexico City. In addition, many homes are improved bit by bit over the years so that what once was a shack, and then a modest house, becomes a quite attractive home with many features in common with those now being sold for very high prices in suburban housing developments. Such is the case in the Campos home, where for years the family lived in a wooden shack on a lot 20 x 60 ft in an outlying neighborhood. Eventually, they replaced the shack with concrete block (*tabique*) walls and have continued to add rooms, and even a second story, in accord with their family finances and needs. While they have made these improvements through a modular approach, many neighbors have done little or nothing to other properties on the block. As a result, the neighborhood, which began thirty years ago as a colonia proletaria, now has a wide range of housing types from low- to middle-income.

Aside from self-improvement as a random mechanism for upgrading homes to middle income standards, the majority of the housing stock available to the growing managerial and professional class has been built in recent years in suburban *fraccionamientos* (subdivisions) with enticing names like "Villa de las Flores." These subdivisions have not yet been the destination of many recent migrants, since most are members of the working classes; but as migrants gain the education and experience to move up the job ladder they become candidates for these housing projects. Several Tzintzuntzan migrants now reside in, or expect their children to live in, these areas. It remains to be seen whether the middle-income suburbs, with their emphasis on "American" style single-

FIG. 3-3—A working-class migrant home located in a northeastern
peripheral neighborhood (1970).

family detached houses and open yards, will create a dilemma
for migrants whose extended family ties are now so important
to their urban lifestyles. In at least a few cases, it is clear that
moving away from other migrants into such suburban developments permits and encourages a breakdown in ties among the
migrants, even among kinsmen. It is curious, when one con-
templates the concern of social scientists, urban planners, and
government officials for the fate of low-income settlements,
that the slums, vecindades, and colonias proletarias may provide a more intensive and satisfying social life than do the
more attractive middle-income homes and apartments.

EDUCATIONAL SYSTEM

Bonilla (1964:192) has pointed out that the "monopoly of
learning in Latin American cities often is an 'explicit' goal of

FIG. 3-4—The same home as in Fig. 3-3, after construction of a second story (1974). This is the Campos home, where the author lives while doing fieldwork in Mexico City.

migration to the city." Despite governmental efforts to raise literacy levels in traditionally backward rural areas, rural schools and teachers remain scarce. Those who seek better education must move to Mexico City or to the few other university centers in Mexico.

In 1960, of the 77,000 students enrolled in institutions of higher learning in Mexico, 68% were in the capital. In 1967, after a significant expansion of state universities, 53% of the 145,000 university students still were in Mexico City's colleges and universities (Lajous Vargas 1968:423). And with the opening of the Universidad Metropolitana in Mexico City in 1974, the concentration of higher education in the capital has increased.

The capital also has the nation's most complete system of primary and secondary schools, both public and private. As a result, there exists a substantial imbalance in educational background between Mexico City residents and those of the rural regions (Table 3-5). Literacy figures also demonstrate the educational superiority of Mexico City's population. In 1930, when the nation was only 33.4% literate, Mexico City

TABLE 3-5
Educational Levels
in Mexico City, Michoacán, and the Nation–1970

Educational Level[1]		Mexico City	Michoacán	Nation
0	years of schooling	16.6	48.1	35.0
1-6	years of schooling	60.9	46.8	55.7
7-9	years of schooling	10.7	3.2	5.1
10-12	years of schooling	3.5	0.7	1.4
13 +	years of schooling	8.3	1.2	2.8
	Totals	100.0	100.0	100.0

[1] Percentage of population 6 years of age and up.

Source: Calculated from figures in IX Censo General de Población (1970), Resumen General 1971:120-121; XXIV-XXV:218-219.

was 67.1% literate; in 1940, in spite of improvements made during the Cárdenas regime, the gap was still large—42.0% vs. 74.0%. Only during the past two decades has the ratio narrowed: in 1950, 57.5% vs. 81.8%; in 1960, 62.2% vs. 83.4%; and in 1970, 76.2% vs. 90.9%. Even with a large immigrant population, Mexico City maintains a substantial lead in literacy over the rest of the nation, thus attracting villagers whose local educational facilities lag behind those in the capital.

COMMUNICATIONS NETWORK

As in nearly all countries with a dominant city, Mexico City is the communications hub of the entire country. It has always been the major focus of new ideas that later diffuse throughout the nation. Spreading out by road, rail, radio, television, and newspapers, the attitudes of *los capitalinos* shape the opinions of rural elites and peasants.

Just as major national highways begin at, and measure distances from, the Zócalo in downtown Mexico City, so do the most important radio and television stations broadcast from the capital. This concentration is not accidental; the government avoids expensive duplication of media facilities by constructing microwave repeater stations throughout the countryside, from the Sonoran desert in the north to the jungles of Chiapas and Yucatán in the south. In this manner, telecommunications are spread over the nation relatively inexpensively and nearly uniformly. Only a few other urban centers, such as Guadalajara, Monterrey, Tijuana, and Ciudad Juarez, have major independent installations (Méndez 1970:141).

The dissemination of urban events through television and radio (and to a lesser degree, magazines and newspapers) permits peasants to know as much, and often more, about Mexico City than they do of events in their own states. Thus, the easily accessible metropolis is well-known to residents in

surrounding regions; and its job opportunities, higher standard of living, educational opportunities, and hectic pace
beckon to and tempt the villager no longer satisfied with his
traditional situation.

SUMMARY

Mexico City is a giant among cities. If New York City had
an equivalent share of the United States population, it would
have more than 35,000,000 inhabitants! This is not to argue
that Mexico City's macrocephalous character is all for the
good. On the contrary, the attractions it has offered in recent
years may be short-lived if current problems are exacerbated
by increased pressures on limited resources of land, water,
electricity, and the like. Just as it is hard to imagine New
York City with 35 million residents, so it is difficult to contemplate what Mexico City might be like if population pro-
jections for the year 2000 come true.

There seems little question, however, that for the present
Mexico City's economic, political, and educational domination of the nation will continue to attract migrants from the
rest of the country. Plans for decentralization offer some
hope, at least to those who design them, but, as Wilkie
(1974:46) has pointed out, "rural workers seem to be increasingly hopeful of finding redemption from peasant
poverty through escape to the big city. . . .Intellectuals are
attracted to the capital because material benefits are lacking
in the provinces." This is as true for the people of Tzintzuntzan as for those in thousands of other Mexican villages
and towns.

CHAPTER 4

THE MIGRANTS: POPULATION AND MOBILITY

The attractions of Mexico City described in the previous chapter are evidence of the forces that have drawn, and continue to draw, peasant migrants to the capital. However, the "push" and "pull" exerted by demographic growth, occupational aspirations, living standards, and educational achievement clearly do not provoke all rural dwellers to abandon their home communities. Often, an additional factor—availability of urban kinship and friendship ties—tips the balance for or against the final decision to migrate, since potential migrants are well aware that they need help locating housing and employment upon arrival in the metropolis or any other urban destination. For Tzintzuntzan peasants now in Mexico City, personal ties with previous migrants from the village provide a substantial motivation at least to risk migration to the capital.

Most Tzintzuntzeños have several potential links that can be activated when they decide to migrate, particularly now that a large and growing population of emigrants is settled in the capital. Upon arrival in Mexico City, most migrants live *arrimado* (i.e., as a "guest") with relatives of friends, and seldom contribute rent or other important components of their own maintenance until they acquire a job. They incur debts, of course; but these are more properly social than monetary and are weighed in the currency of customary interpersonal ties rather than in the coin of modern economics. The period of dependency usually ends as the new migrant settles into the first job and seeks separate quarters to live in. If he is married and has not already brought his wife and children to the city, now will be the occasion for reuniting the family in the capital. In many ways, therefore, the use of these personal networks lowers the economic, social, and psychological costs of departing the village for the urban setting.

THE MIGRANT POPULATION

Considering the recentness of most Tzintzuntzeño migration to Mexico City, there are a great many emigrants now residing in the capital. According to my 1970 ethnographic census, the migrants and their families totaled at least 483 persons. This population consisted of 246 full-time permanent Tzintzuntzeño migrants plus another 38 part-time emigrants. In addition, the migrant households contained 39 spouses born elsewhere, 116 children born in Mexico City, 24 children born enroute to the capital, 10 non-Tzintzuntzan relatives, and 10 non-Tzintzuntzan friends.

In 1970, the migrants were distributed among more than 40 *colonias* or neighborhoods, with most concentrated in the northern parts of the metropolis (see Fig. 4-1). The major concentrations were in the northeastern periphery, especially in colonias such as Gabriel Hernandez, in the far western colonia of Los Remedios, and in other peripheral zones away from the traditional central city slums.

According to my follow-up census survey of 1974, at least 629 Tzintzuntzeños (or their affines) lived in Mexico City just four years after my initial fieldwork. This represents an increase of 23% over the total of 483 migrants in 1970. By 1974, there were at least 105 household units, of which I was able to census directly some 65 and to gather secondary data on the remainder. (In addition, there are still a few households about which I have no more than the name of the family head.) For those households on which I do have reliable information—there were 378 persons born in Tzintzuntzan or its municipio, 55 spouses born elsewhere, 176 children born elsewhere (nearly always in the capital), 10 in-laws born elsewhere, and another 10 friends from other places. As

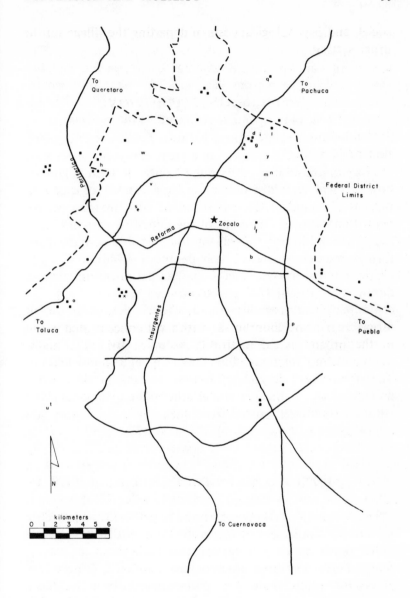

FIG. 4-1–Locations of Tzintzuntzan migrants in Mexico City: 1970.

a consequence, the migrant households tended to be rather large, especially for their usually cramped living quarters. The average migrant household contained 5.9 persons, and the largest reached 13 persons. The most frequent sizes were—four persons (16%), two persons (14%), five persons (12%), seven persons (11%), and a single individual (10%). These sizes accounted for nearly two-thirds of all migrant households (Fig. 4-2).

In a fashion similar to 1970, the Tzintzuntzeños in Mexico City in 1974 were distributed among a number of colonias. Indeed, their dispersion had increased so as to cover more than fifty colonias. The bulk of the migrants were still to be found in the northern half of the metropolis, with even further distances between their peripheral locations and the center of the city (see Fig. 4-3). The pattern of movement during the 1969-1970 period was an extension of the center-peripheral mobility trend, though few migrants in recent years have lived in the urban core region. This niche in the urban system is already occupied by earlier, non-Tzintzuntzeño migrants, their children, and grandchildren. Therefore, the Tzintzuntzeños now arriving in the capital move directly to the peripheral zones where they can take advantage of their predecessors' locations near factory job opportunities.

INTRA-METROPOLITAN GEOGRAPHICAL MOBILITY

Until recently, few ethnographers have tried to explain the patterns and processes of intra-urban residential movements. Most studies of geographical mobility have been short-term but attempt to compensate by emphasizing a life history approach. Nonetheless, the dynamics of decision-making among migrants tend to be obscured, particularly since migrants make choices in the context of changing metropolitan environments. As cities expand, their peripheries enlarge; and

FIG. 4-2—Two middle-class migrant families.

so do the options of migrants who seek to have their own homes rather than renting a place to live.

My first fieldwork in 1969 and 1970 generated migration histories for more than 40 families and individual migrants. The overall pattern was that the earlier arrivals (in the 1940s and 1950s) had settled in slum zones near the center of Mexico City (Fig. 4-4). As they improved their socio-economic circumstances, they tended to move to the periphery, especially in the northeast quadrant of the metropolis. Later arrivals (1960s) tended to move directly to the periphery with the assistance of those who had already located there (Fig. 4-5). These migrants have tended to move even farther out from the city's center as the metropolitan zone expanded and new peripheral zones became available for settlement (through legal subdivisions, quasi-legal neighborhoods, or illegal squatter settlements).

The most recent (1970s) migrants often proceed directly from Tzintzuntzan to the city's outskirts where they settle initially with friends or relatives and then subsequently search for their own apartments. High rents and cramped living conditions in the central city as well as difficulty of transportation to distant factories and difficulty of access to previous arrivals' hospitality have combined to alter the earlier pattern of contact with the urban environment.

This change has important consequences for urban adaptation. While social relationships between residents of traditional *barrios* in the central city tend to be almost as frequent and intense as those of "closed" rural communities (Lewis 1965:495), these people are effectively isolated from factory employment opportunities concentrated primarily on the urban periphery. Thus, Tzintzuntzeños now arriving in the capital benefit economically by moving directly to the periphery, although their social relationships beyond the immediate family may be diminished until they are more permanently settled.

Choice of residence is nearly always influenced by knowledge gained from one's fellow migrants. In order to find inexpensive housing in "safe" areas, recent arrivals depend on the counsel of those more familiar with available opportunities. It is not surprising, then, that most migrants settle in the immediate vicinity of other migrants or in a neighborhood where those individuals formerly resided. Ideally, Tzintzuntzeños desire to live near other migrants and close to their place of employment or near a bus route that reaches it.

Obviously, Tzintzuntzeños do not form an "urban village" in Mexico City. The arrival of migrants at different times, their different housing needs, and their different occupations have combined to disperse these migrants. Moreover, the overcrowded housing market effectively prevents any large group from forming a single neighborhood cluster unless they purchase or invade marginal lands without access to transportation, water, electricity, and sewage. Thus, each migrant family must use its own resources within and beyond the migrant group to resolve its housing needs.

The uneven geographic dispersal of Tzintzuntzeños in Mexico City also reflects their entry near the lower end of the urban economic hierarchy. They tend to cluster in working-class neighborhoods and to avoid the stifling conditions of the slums. Furthermore, upward economic mobility is paralleled by the migrants' search for better housing.

While geographical separation in Mexico City destroys much of the migrants' traditional sense of "community" identification, propinquity per se does not induce interaction among migrants who lack kinship ties, who are of unequal socioeconomic status, or who have lived in the city for different lengths of time. An example may illustrate. Five migrant households are located in one neighborhood in the city's northeast sector. Three are located on the same block and contain young migrants with kinship ties, common occupations, and similar short-term urban exposure. The other two are located three blocks away; they are related to each other by kinship ties, occupations, and long-term urban

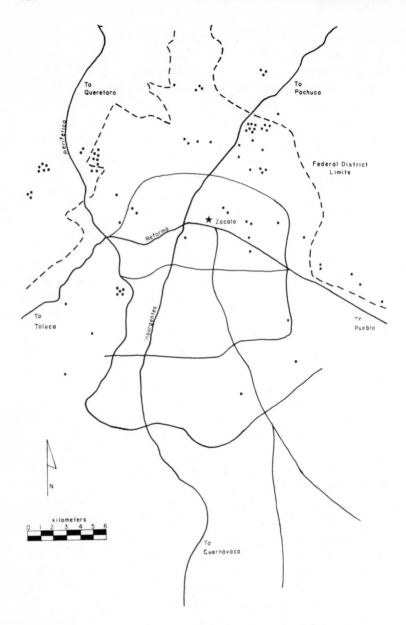

FIG. 4-3–Locations of Tzintzuntzan migrants in Mexico City: 1974.

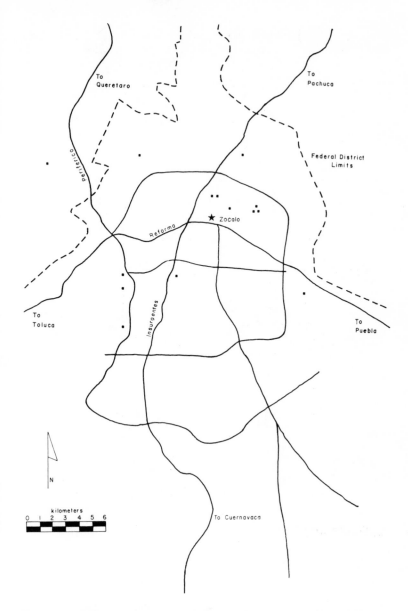

FIG. 4-4—Locations of first residence of migrants who arrived in
Mexico City before 1960.

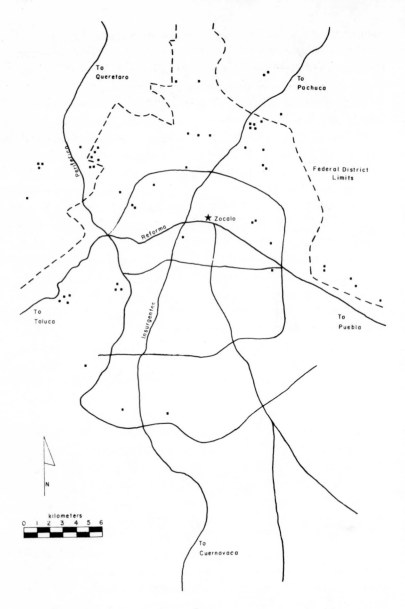

FIG. 4-5—Locations of first residence of migrants who arrived in Mexico City after 1960.

residence. Although the two groups are aware of the presence of the other in the same neighborhood, interaction between them is virtually non-existent. In other words, in the single neighborhood are two migrant enclaves, not one.

An important adjunct of geographical separation is the virtual absence of automobiles and telephones among Tzintzuntzan migrants in the city. Most migrants view distance as a major hindrance to retaining the levels of social interaction taken for granted in the village. Personal visits are the principal means for conducting migrant social intercourse; but the great distances, sometimes requiring two-hour bus trips, combine with the absence of alternate means of communication to severely limit its frequency and intensity. Under such conditions, the nuclear household and extended-family enclave become the most important sources of social interaction and economic security for Tzintzuntzan migrants.

Frequent changes in urban location also curtail social relations among many Tzintzuntzeños in Mexico City. Finding some migrant households is impossible because no one has up-to-date information regarding their locations. Furthermore, several migrants have isolated themselves to escape revenge by villagers or capture by police for crimes committed in Tzintzuntzan.

As a result of this process, and of the patterns of job search after arrival, I hypothesize that a series of "enclaves" are now developing among the Tzintzuntzan migrants. Some evidence for this was gathered during the 1974 field season. In one case, I discovered that while in 1969 and 1970 only two families (related by marriage) lived in Xalpa, a northwestern-sector neighborhood, in 1974 some 11 families resided in this neighborhood. Every family drawn into this "enclave," which covers an area within a five-minute walk, shared ties of kinship, *compadrazgo*, or urban working-place. As the "enclave" developed, the ties among the families were strengthened at the expense of ties with the remainder of the Tzintzuntzeños in the capital. By 1976, as some of these Xalpa residents were buying lots for homes on the extreme western metropolitan periphery, the enclave was splintering. Thus, it appears that these "enclaves" are likely to be transitory mechanisms of urban adaptation which will endure only until their members are able to break away in the search for their own homes. As I continue the fieldwork into the next decade, I will be in a position to test the "enclave" hypothesis by collecting information on the residential choices made by the continuing flow of Tzintzuntzeños to the capital.

TZINTZUNTZAN MIGRANTS AND THE TURNER THEORY

The data available on the intra-metropolitan movements of the Tzintzuntzan migrants offer us the opportunity to evaluate the theory, suggested in the writings of John Turner (1965, 1967, 1968), that rural-urban migrants tend to settle initially in the central city region and then subsequently move to the periphery after a period of adjustment to urban life. More specifically, Turner argues that migrants are concerned initially with the location of their housing, subsequently with their security of tenure, and ultimately with the amenities available in their homes. The bulk of evidence gathered by Turner in Lima, Peru, and in other cities in the developing countries, appears to uphold this processual model of migrant assimilation into the urban milieu.

On the other hand, the experiences of the Tzintzuntzeños in Mexico City suggests that the Turner theory may be applicable only in certain cultural-historical circumstances in the urbanizing countries. For instance, it appears that the earliest Tzintzuntzan migrants to arrive in the capital did, indeed, settle in or near the central city area before becoming sufficiently familiar with the urban setting and adequately secure in their job situations that they took the risk of moving to the periphery, at least as the city's edge then existed. Later arrivals took a clue from those who had gone ahead and moved more directly to the periphery or intermediate zones and, in the process, avoided the central city slums altogether. Recent circumstances of high rents, rent control, and expanding factory work opportunities in peripheral industrial zones made the Tzintzuntzeños' decision to move directly from the village to the urban periphery a logical choice. As the periphery continued (and continues today) to move away from the central city zone, so the migrants also extended their range, until now they can be found at distances of up to 15 or 20 km from downtown. In these terms, it is not surprising that Lewis (1952) found the bulk of Tepoztecan migrants located in central city slums, whereas I found most Tzintzuntzan migrants dispersed near the periphery. The transformation and expansion of the metropolitan area over 25 years has substantially altered the housing and employment niches open to new migrant arrivals and to those who succeed in the urban economic competition (Fig. 4-6).

The variation in the intra-urban mobility experiences of Tzintzuntzan migrants and those studied earlier by Lewis in Mexico City is supported by two additional field studies in contemporary Mexico City. Both Brown (1972) and Jackson (1973) have concluded that recent working-class migrants to Mexico City exhibit behavior similar to that of the Tzintzuntzeños. Jackson observes that "Perhaps the migration process has progressed to a point where incoming migrants have contacts in peripheral areas in sufficient numbers to permit many to skip the stage of living in downtown vecindades" (1973:94); and Brown argues that " . . . in the Mexican case . . . in part because of rent control, the central city slums, or tugurios as they are called, house few recent migrants and that residential stability in these districts today is one of the highest in the metropolitan area" (1972:166-167).

FIG. 4-6—Two working-class migrant homes on the periphery of Mexico City. Both are next door to houses owned by relatives and thus form enclaves.

SUMMARY

In recent years, the population of Tzintzuntzan migrants in Mexico City has continued to expand both in numbers and in geographical extent. As the population has grown, a pattern of enclaves—composed of kinsmen, compadres, and close friends from the village—has developed. These enclaves are fragile entities subject to the vagaries of intra-urban mobility patterns. The success of the earlier migrants in establishing a bridgehead in the capital has enabled more recent arrivals to take advantage of residential and employment opportunities that may not be available even to the urban natives. This reflects once more the great importance of personal networks in the urbanization process in which the Tzintzuntzan migrants are involved.

CHAPTER 5

HOUSEHOLD AND FAMILY ORGANIZATION

In the preceding chapters we have described the patterns, causes, and consequences of migration from Tzintzuntzan to Mexico City. In this chapter we turn to those aspects of migrant urban adaptation which involve family and household organization, the roles and statuses of persons within the family, and the functions of the family in the urban setting. Through census and ethnographic data we will see how rural family and household patterns are modified within the urban situation in Mexico City.

Before describing the migrant situation in Mexico City, it is appropriate to summarize the main features of family and household structure in Tzintzuntzan (see Foster 1967:55-59). In 1970, the village population was divided among 360 households, of which 252 (70%) were nuclear, 59 (16.4%) were joint, and the remaining 49 (13.6%) were "truncated."[1] These three household categories contained 371 married couples plus the 49 truncated units, for a total of 420 families. Despite recent demographic pressures on a limited land and housing supply, 88% of the villagers reside in their own homes. Renting and caretaking are gradually becoming more important, however, as emigrants leave behind empty houses and the urban elite from the state capital build summer houses on the shores of Lake Pátzcuaro near Tzintzuntzan.

Although the nuclear bilateral family is the most significant socioeconomic unit in the village and most households are composed of a single conjugal family unit, it is a rare Tzintzuntzeño who never resides in a household containing two or more families during his lifetime. This is due to local inheritance practices and to a preference for post-marital patrilocal residence. In such a setting, the joint household often serves as a transitional phase in which some combination of cooking and budget arrangements bring together two siblings' families or the families of parents and sons (Nutini 1967:390). The truncated household, by contrast, results not from choice or expediency but from circumstances of death or separation and thus creates an imbalance between family needs and their ability to meet them. Under all conditions, extended family ties are usually weak and sometimes lacking completely.

In sum, as Tzintzuntzan peasants grow up, marry, have children, and eventually watch them depart, they usually belong to a series of nuclear, joint, and truncated households. These correspond to the requirements of different segments of the typical peasant family developmental cycle and, as such, constitute complementary rather than antithetical aspects of village social life.

With this brief description of village patterns in mind, we now consider the family and household structure of Tzintzuntzan migrants in Mexico City.

FAMILY AND HOUSEHOLD

The migrant household population is divided into 71 (67.6%) nuclear households, 9 (8.6%) joint households, and 25 (23.8%) "truncated" households. The proportion of nuclear households is approximately the same as it is in Tzintzuntzan. However, there are fewer joint households—based on co-residence—and more "truncated" households. The increase in this last category reflects the large number of young migrants who have come to the capital to attend secondary schools, seminaries, convents, preparatory schools, and universities. The influx of temporary guests, both relatives and friends, in migrant homes combines with a continuing high birth rate (and a low level of infant mortality) to generate a mean household size of 5.9 persons. This is slightly lower than in Tzintzuntzan, where the average is 6.2 persons.

FIG. 5-1—A government housing project where a middle-class migrant family rents an apartment (*above*); a private condominium development where another middle-class family owns an apartment (*below*).

NUCLEAR HOUSEHOLDS AND
EXTENDED FAMILIES

Comparison of village and migrant household structure might lead us to conclude that the joint family declines in importance in the urbanization process while the nuclear and "truncated" types become more significant. This has been widely regarded as an inevitable consequence of worldwide urbanization. However, analysis of the role of the extended family shows the narrowness of such a viewpoint.

When kinship-related families live in the same *vecindad* or even in the same neighborhood, they often share many important domestic and social activities. By reanalyzing the data on Tzintzuntzeños in Mexico City, I discovered that the incidence of these "extended family enclaves" (Leeds and Leeds 1970) is relatively high. For the 65 households which I censused directly, more than half (33 of 65) belong to extended family units.[2] Moreover, of the 22 nuclear families living in relative isolation from the other migrants, 14 contain relatives beyond the basic husband, wife, and children combination. Thus, the *isolated* nuclear family is the exception rather that the rule among Tzintzuntzan migrants in Mexico City.

For the majority of Tzintzuntzeños in the capital, extended families serve as significant aspects of their urban adaptation. New arrivals are not limited to a single family unit in the search for housing and employment. They also may turn to a wider set of kinsmen living in the immediate vicinity of the family with whom they are living.

JOINT HOUSEHOLDS

Although there are only seven joint households among the 65 migrant households I censused, their differences from the rural patterns show how the urban setting influences the

FIG. 5-2—A vecindad in the northwestern zone of Mexico City. From 1973 to 1976, four related migrant families lived here; in 1976 two families bought a lot and built houses on it in the far western edge of the city.

organization of apparently similar social forms. Urban joint households develop in two main ways. Among poor families sharing cramped quarters in order to stretch otherwise insufficient incomes, they grow by accretion in response to urban housing availability. Thus, a truncated household may become a nuclear household, then a joint household, and may split again into two nuclear households forming an extended family enclave.

Joint households also occur among more affluent Tzintzuntzeños in the city. With these families, co-residence and sharing of domestic functions arise not from their need to dilute the effect of poverty but from parental desire to inculcate proper behavior in their newlywed sons and daughters-in-law. This type of joint household resembles the traditional village pattern more than does the type described above. In fact, only those migrants who own homes or rent apartments large enough to comfortably contain two or more families attempt to create such joint households.

Nevertheless, all migrants do follow a universal rule; they form joint households only among kinsmen. Thus, the joint household among Tzintzuntzeños in Mexico City does not result from attempts to recreate traditional rural residence patterns. In fact, the rarity of the joint household and the large number of renters attests to the tightness of Mexico City's housing market.[3]

TRUNCATED HOUSEHOLDS

Among Tzintzuntzan migrants in Mexico City, truncated households occur in several situations. First, desertion or separation often causes a spouse (with or without children) to migrate to Mexico City. Domestic servants also form an important segment of truncated households. Third, widowed parents sometimes follow their children to the capital. Finally, young adults sometimes establish independent residences after a period of living with kinsmen. In addition, a number of students have been sent by their parents to attend boarding schools in the capital.

Thus, truncated households are an important modification of traditional Tzintzuntzan family and residence patterns in the urban setting: occupational and educational requirements usually determine the urban type; death, separation, or emigration produce the rural counterpart. Of course, truncated households are generally transitional, since marriage and subsequent intra-urban movements shift individuals into nuclear or joint household categories.

MATRIFOCAL FAMILIES AMONG TZINTZUNTZAN MIGRANTS

The literature on working-class families in Latin American cities suggests the prevalence of the "matrifocal family" or "female-based household," in which kin relations emphasize the female line; the husband (if present) assumes a marginal position in the economic survival of the household and in the children's daily discipline; and the transient relations between husbands and wives can be described as serial monogamy or even serial polyandry (e.g., Gonzalez 1965, 1969; Lewis 1965; Peattie 1968; Safa 1964). The principal causes for the male's limited role are job insecurity (due to lack of adequate education, job skills, and opportunities for upward mobility) and the woman's ability to support the family through self-employment in domestic services, which further weakens and threatens the male's position as chief economic provider and *jefe de familia* (Patch 1961:20).

In contrast, the matrifocal family is rare among Tzintzuntzeños in Mexico City. Several woman (widows with children or abandoned mothers with children) do head households, but only twice have women formed *uniones libres* with more than one husband. Female-headed households lacking steady male employment or suffering underemployment do appear among the Tzintzuntzeños in Mexico City; however, only the few domestic servants fall into that category.

Since the matrifocal family is rare among Tzintzuntzan migrants in Mexico City, what accounts for the predominance of its opposite—the bilateral conjugal household? I believe that the prevalence of steady male employment provides men with statuses and roles which stabilize the marital relationship. In Tzintzuntzan and other villages, where the peasant household represents the basic production unit, male employment is high, and male-dominated nuclear households are the rule. Although work is performed outside the migrant household, employment rates for husbands are surprisingly high, with the result that the matrifocal family does not flourish.

INTERPERSONAL RELATIONS
IN THE MIGRANT FAMILY

Husbands and Wives

As we have seen, the conjugal family, whether manifest in the nuclear household or in the extended family enclave, predominates among Tzintzuntzeños in Mexico City. However, analysis of family and household structure reveals little about the quality of interpersonal relations among family members. In Tzintzuntzan, "Villagers are in general agreement about ideal role behavior within the family: the husband is dominant, owed obedience and respect by his wife and children even after the latter reach adulthood. The wife should be faithful and submissive, frugal and careful in managing family resources, and kind and loving with her children" (Foster 1967:59).

Such attitudes are reflected in the traditional division of labor in peasant families; as the saying goes, *el hombre en la*

FIG. 5-3–Contrasting lifestyles for migrant women: a domestic servant and her granddaughter at the home of her employer (*above*); a school principal with her young husband, her new car, and her weekend house (*below*).

plaza, y la mujer en la casa. Migrant attitudes toward ideal role behavior and proper division of labor between spouses vary considerably from the traditional Tzintzuntzan view. To be sure, husbands are the principal participants in the urban wage labor market, while their wives remain responsible for the smooth functioning of the household. But, husbands (as well as male children) often also perform such tasks as sweeping patios, washing dishes, and tending younger children. Such active and willing participation in household tasks, rare in Tzintzuntzan, shows that migrant men are neither helplessly dependent on their wives nor concerned about loss of "masculinity" (Leñero Otero 1968:132-133).

For instance, among the young bachelors who have spent time in Mexico City to complete their education, the ethic of male dominance is largely replaced by a belief in marital democracy which allows women equal authority and responsibility in the family affairs (Leñero Otero 1968:134). Furthermore, according to this "modern" attitude, wives may even continue in their careers after marriage. Thus, a preoccupation with economic success may override the traditional attitude that a woman's place is in the home.

Relations between spouses in migrant families are also significantly influenced by the absence of the groom's mother, who in the Tzintzuntzan peasant family exercises control over a son's wife when the newlyweds live in her home. The mother-in-law traditionally is considered a hard taskmaster who exploits her son's wife and thereby creates serious strains between herself, her son, and his wife. But when the mother-in-law is absent, as she usually is among migrant families, relations between husband and wife tend to be more egalitarian from the outset. Thus, separation from village and husband's mother liberates the migrant wife from much of her traditional suffering and exploitation (Esteva Fabregat 1969:205).

However, as the case of the Zavala family demonstrates, traditional tensions occur when the mother-in-law is present.

Although José strongly believes that it is "unfair and unwise to have one's married children in the household because of the inevitable domination of the young couple and their children," his wife convinced him that their son Victor should bring his new wife to stay with the family for "at least six months," so that she could "get to know the girl and help correct some errors in her conduct, her domestic skills, and her attitudes toward marriage." As Victor remarked somewhat bitterly, "My wife knows how to cook, to iron clothes, and sew—but only in her own style. My mother has to be sure that she does everything the right way!"

Responses to the Thematic Apperception Test and data from life histories provide additional insights into sensitive areas of husband-wife relationships. An example of the former reveals a basically egalitarian relationship between spouses.

CARD 4—A young woman is clutching the shoulders of a man whose face and body are averted as if he were trying to pull away from her.

NARRATOR—A 48-year-old married man

I have always felt that in addition to dedicating oneself to a career, one should share happiness with his wife. . . .To me, my wife has been like my second half, with myself as the first half. We have struggled through life together, in happy times and in suffering, and we hope to have a happy future. . . .One improves himself, but not alone, rather always with the support of his wife. What is a wife if not a help-mate? For me, the wife is no slave, but has her own principles—just like the husband—and her own obligations and makes her own mistakes, all of which should be recognized and shared together. . . .This is my intention: to have a stable future so that I can share my happiness and success with my wife, who is the only person who has suffered with me through all my disappointments and through my happiness.

His wife's life history is replete with references to her reasons for marrying José, to their attitudes toward each other and toward their children, and to their aspirations and ambitions for the future in the context of equitable marital relations:

After I married José, everyone in Tzintzuntzan criticized me and wanted to know why I, a widow with two children, would be interested in him. I replied that I wanted to marry someone who would bring up the children correctly, would take me out of Quiroga where I was living in the house of my deceased husband, would take good care of me, and would see to the children's education. And besides, we had been *novios* at an early age and had always liked each other, despite my marriage at age 13 to an elderly man from Quiroga and despite José's departure to Morelia to finish his education. He could have married someone else, just as I might have done, but I rejected several other suitors because my interest was in the betterment of myself and my children, and José's career and his personal concern appeared to offer a sound base for our future. He has always respected me, without regard to the property left to me by my first husband; he wanted our relationship to be based on love and understanding, not on material goods. José and I always come to an agreement on our problems, whether it is over money or our plans, or vacations, or clothes purchases, or our food and meals. We share things between us so that we can achieve our goals in life without falling into debt or suffering unduly. In fact, we have lived well, have had no difficulties to speak of, and have gotten as far in life as our money would take us.

In sum, husband-wife relations in migrant families tend to be egalitarian and mutually supportive: most men assist and cooperate in domestic chores, and progressive, younger women are career- as well as family-oriented. Regardless of their specific arrangements for income production and domestic duties, nearly all families demonstrate a low level of male authoritarianism and a high degree of "democratic" conflict resolution between spouses. Clearly, the saying, *el consejo de la mujer es poco y el que no le toma es loco* ("women's advice is of little value, but only a fool would ignore it"), better expresses the tension between ideal and actual behavior between spouses in Tzintzuntzan households than in migrant households.

Parents and Children

If the great triangle of adulthood in Tzintzuntzan peasant families is husband, wife, and mother-in-law, then the major triad of childhood is mother, father, and child. In the traditional Mexican peasant family, males assert their masculinity by adopting the role of *El Macho* ("the He-Man"), while females fall in the opposing role of *la madre abnegada* ("the long-suffering mother").[4]

Among Tzintzuntzan migrants in Mexico City, however, fathers are more apt to be affectionate toward their children, open and understanding in their counsel, eager to labor for their children's betterment, and concerned with being a friend rather than a symbol of ultimate authority—that is, they tend to reject behavior associated with rural *machismo*. Again, TAT responses illustrate several important elements of these migrant attitudes: the first story demonstrates a perceptive understanding—and a rejection—of the traditional relationship between father and children; the second provides guidelines for more effective father-child relations; and the third shows how fathers and their children should jointly resolve their difficulties in order to turn suffering into success, poverty into progress.

CARD 7BM—A gray-haired man is looking at a younger man who is sullenly staring into space.

NARRATOR—26-year-old bachelor

The mother is always idolized, and is considered very different from her husband. Children feel that the parents do not have the same affection for their own children, but upon a bit of reflection we realize that the father, in spite of not showing affection in the open manner of the mother, may love us, even more than she does. This can be better explained by example. There was a family formed, like all families, by the parents and children. In this family the father always felt restrained. Whenever the children assembled, he found some way to separate himself from the group. Despite this, he felt that he loved his children more than their own mother did, but the children did not respond. Once, a son noticed his attitude, approached him, and inquired as to why the father always retired from these family gatherings. The father replied that he felt inferior since all the children's affection was directed at his wife. The son, who loved his father, confessed this feeling of affection to his father, and made him understand that the children loved the father just as much as the mother, but that they couldn't demonstrate it as directly since the mother—being of the opposite sex—could receive their affection in a more direct form than the father. From then on, the father understood the children's attitudes and ever since has always participated in all the family gatherings.

NARRATOR—48-year-old man

When one has children, there is no better way to guide them than through the example of one's own behavior. The children take up many good habits from the father; if one is exacting at home, then they learn a habit valuable in their education and for their role in society.

How many times does a child ask advice of his father? But there are times when he is not brave enough to ask the father for counsel. In that case, the father must be a friend to his child. There can be no better friend than a father. The father should be a friend, not just an authority figure. . .

The father gives his all to his children and wants them to enjoy life to the fullest. What is very important is for the father to be a man of strong principles, to understand life, and to take part in the resolution of the world's problems, so that through such principles he may benefit the progress of his children.

NARRATOR—18-year-old bachelor

For the past 15 years the father had been without a wife and the son without a mother. During this time, they had been very poor, but the father was a hard worker who hated vice as much as he strived to bring about a good future for his son. The son was put in school, and the father labored to pay for it until the son finished. The son also worked to help pay for his studies. They had many adventures together, but since they were so poor they sometimes went hungry and went without sleep because they always worked so hard and so much. So, the son studied hard, thought about the future, a future when he would accomplish something because of his studies. And his father thought the same thing, and kept helping his son. So, the son studied until he was named President of the Republic. And he felt satisfied at having achieved what he thought about. And they were happy, and the son married and so did the father—and they all lived together and were very happy.

What accounts for such different views of father-child ties among traditional peasant families and Tzintzuntzan migrants? First, the absence of the man's mother relieves him from playing the conflicting roles of son and husband at the same time. Consequently, the authoritarianism of village fathers, expressed through *machismo*, can be replaced by closer emotional ties between father and children. For example, child-beating is common in Tzintzuntzan but is rare among the migrants in Mexico city. Discipline in the city seems rather lax, in fact, with rebukes most often limited to

mild verbal urgings for proper behavior. One man percep-
tively remarked that his wife should discipline their children
when they misbehaved during the day; he did not relish returning home each night to enforce discipline long after an
incident had been forgotten. Besides, he pointed out, this
would make him an authoritarian disliked by his children,
whereas by not scolding them the wife would remain their
friend and advocate!

Traditional machismo also has economic referent (see
Swartzbaugh 1970:5). Peasant fathers retreat to public decla-
rations of their masculinity, often expressed through authoritarianism, self-isolation and defensiveness, and drinking,
when their actual accomplishments are severely constrained
by ecological and economic forces (Esteva Fabregat 1969:
222 ff.). That is, adoption of the symbols of El Macho allows
males to establish a "social front" (Nelson 1971:74) by
which they can avoid ultimate responsibility for their failure
to properly provide for their families.

Among Tzintzuntzeños in Mexico City, a father provides
daily evidence of his manhood through his stable and
continuing economic contributions to his family's prosperity, and so exchanges—at least symbolically—the traditional machismo behavior for a preferred status within
the family group. Nearly all migrant men reject the ethic of
machismo as unreasonable, disreputable, *sin urbanidad*
("uneducated"), and associate it with the rural traditions
they abandoned.[5]

Although migrant males tend to slough off the symbols
and reject the model of El Macho, females retain much of
their traditional status as the long suffering and self-
sacrificing mother, la madre abnegada, who is particularly
associated with the struggle to cope with poverty, both rural
and urban, in Mexican society.[6] Perhaps no better exemplifi-
cation of her quantities, attitudes, and devotion to her children can be found than in the following TAT narrative,
which was told in response to the *blank* card.

CARD 16—Blank card.

NARRATOR—26-year-old bachelor

We will call this story "The Mother," without regard to her nationality, simply the mother. I will speak about the mother from the moment in which she becomes one, that is, from the time she has children who bear her name. La madre abnegada, like all mothers everywhere, in order to achieve this position has to pass through several stages—the first is to find the proper husband.

The mother about whom I speak was a poor mother, and for that reason she married another poor person. The first years were happy since their poverty didn't bother them. They had a child, then another, and then came the economic problems that naturally come to poor couples. The father, trying to achieve the happiness he desired—not just for himself, but for all the family members—had to leave to look for work since there was none where they lived. He left, and the mother never heard from him again. Thus began her suffering and anxiety since she now had to provide her children with food. The place where they lived was poor and unhealthy, and they suffered from the inclement weather during the rainy season. A river near the home overflowed and everyone in the village, including themselves, had to flee. They fled, and came to unknown places where they suffered even more than previously.

But, the strength of the mother to achieve the impossible carried the family forward, and after much suffering she managed to see her children grow to adulthood and to give them the education she wished for them. A life full of pains finally brought success. It brought the final result she hoped for in that she saw her children achieve what she had hoped for them—a marriage, a marriage that achieved the happiness that she had never had until many years later.

In families dominated by machismo-oriented fathers, the mother struggles to overcome his lack of support in raising the children and instilling in them her values and attitudes. In contrast, among nearly all Tzintzuntzan families in Mexico City, there exists a strong bond between spouses that is at once egalitarian and mutually supportive. The steady economic contribution of the husband permits the wife to devote full attention to bringing up the children in the unfamiliar urban setting. The mother, therefore, retains a strong link to her children, but her suffering and sacrifice are not expressive and manipulative, but instrumental and achievement-oriented; she struggles, in cooperation with her husband, to assure her children a better place in the future by easing their progress over the hurdles which impede economic and social mobility in the city.

The reaction of children to this reinterpretation of the role of la madre abnegada is equivocal: on the one hand, they continue to show deep-seated attachment to their mothers; on the other, while aware that they ought not to abuse their mothers, they believe that no matter what occurs she will always accept them back. The following TAT narratives illustrate these two attitudes toward the mother in the migrant family.

CARD 15—A gaunt man with clenched hands is standing among gravestones.

NARRATOR—20-year-old bachelor

Since childhood, his mother, whom he deeply loved, had been dead. On the night she had been buried, he had cried a lot and asked himself why this had to happen to him. After she was buried he spent nearly the whole next day at the grave. Days passed and each day he visited his mother's grave to ask her to take care of him and to help him. For him his only dream was to contemplate his mother's tomb, and he believed that the only thing that kept him from doing this was death. And, he wanted death to come soon for him so that he could be reunited with his mother and again see her as he did when he was a boy.

CARD 6BM—A short elderly woman stands with her back turned to a tall young man. The latter is looking downward with a perplexed expression.

NARRATOR—26-year-old bachelor

In one of the many Colonias in Mexico City, lived a family formed by a mother and several children, but the father had died sometime ago. In this family there was a young man who made excessive demands on his mother, especially economic demands that she, being alone, was unable to satisfy. He fled in disgust in the belief that he could find elsewhere what he wanted. After wandering through unknown regions, he realized that he couldn't find what he had demanded. So, after a while, after suffering many difficulties, he returned home to ask forgiveness from his mother. His mother, like all mothers anywhere, felt happy and accepted him back, even though he had made her suffer and made her feel incapable of giving him what he wanted. After this, the young man behaved differently; he changed totally and instead of making demands, he got a job which gave him the satisfaction he desired and also brought him the affection of his mother.

The relationship between mother and children, then, is one of great *confianza* ("trust" and "intimacy"), in which she must try to teach her children proper behavior without converting them into puppets subject to her manipulative skills. The balance in the migrant home is struck between mother, father, and children; when all runs smoothly, the mother is highly revered by all, the father can stand proudly by her side because of his important role as economic provider, and the children are socialized in an atmosphere which allows them to develop their full potential for later success in urban life.

The proper resolution of the conflict between traditional family role models and those in most migrant families is aptly expressed by the following TAT response:

CARD 6BM—Elderly woman with tall young man.

NARRATOR—48-year-old married man

The mother is a second element in the home. In general, Mexicans do not pay enough attention to the mother: they relegate her to secondary status, and give primary importance to the father. She is not consulted; at times even has no rights in her own home. This is bad and should be corrected—the mother should have her rights as well as her obligations. . .The mother obviously should have much confianza with her children and should also be their friend. A friendly mother can resolve many problems, she should set a good example for her children to follow. The mother should not be a dictator but should ask herself what is best for the children. The mother is so important that we must not mistreat her; she is always an object of our love and affection. Even when we die, the word "mother" is on our lips, and is our own special benediction.

SUMMARY

In this chapter we examined family and household structure among Tzintzuntzan migrants in Mexico City. We have shown that the conjugal family remains at the center of the migrants' lives. The nuclear household becomes less important as the extended family and "truncated" household types have emerged as new forms in the urban setting.

The quality of interpersonal relationships within migrant families is also affected by urbanization. Husband-wife and parent-child rapport improves as males slough off the "social front" of machismo, women reinterpret the role of la madre abnegada, and children grow up in an environment stressing independence and achievement. Furthermore, the absence of the husband's mother and his steady economic contributions in migrant households result in a more egalitarian family.

Thus, urbanization has wrought changes subtle and profound in the family life of Tzintzuntzeños in Mexico City. So far these changes have been overwhelmingly integrative rather than disorganizing. At a time when Latin American urbanization proceeds at a dizzying pace, the positive role played by the migrant family certainly demands our attention. Indeed, in its role as "an institution prevailing over rapid change" (Carlos and Seller 1972:114), the migrant family serves as a flexible vehicle for social and economic progress.

Notes for Chapter Five

1. In distinguishing between family and household, I follow Bender (1967:495), who notes that family and household are logically distinct because the referent of the former is kinship, that of the latter, residence. Furthermore, he points out that the concept of household embodies two complementary, but separate, variables: co-residence and domestic functions. On the basis of these distinctions, four theoretical types are possible: Independent Nuclear Households; Joint Domestic Groups; Joint Residence Groups; and Joint Households. Thus, a nuclear household refers to a married couple (with or without children), while a joint household contains two or more married couples (with or without children) sharing co-residence and domestic functions. A "truncated" household is defined here as a residence group in which no married couple is present.

2. On the basis of fieldwork in a Oaxaca urban barrio, Chance (1971:133) found that: "Once household and family are clearly distinguished, the incidence of the nuclear family as a kinship unit is seen to be relatively low, since many units which are commonly classified as families are in fact components of larger extended family groupings which may include three or more (usually nuclear) households. In contrast, the incidence of the extended families is significantly higher."

3. Of course, few migrant families yet have children over age 18, so that the formation of joint households is more properly a matter for

future research than for present speculation.

4. Nelson (1971:71) describes the differences between El Macho and la madre abnegada in these words: "The mother is open, receptive, passive, submissive; El Macho is impenetrable, closed within himself, capable of guarding himself and what is his, defensive, dominating, unpredictable, and arbitrary."

5. Macho behavior is common among the poorest urban families, for whom the daily struggle for survival is scarcely less intense than for rural peasants. The work of Lewis (1959) illustrates clearly the importance of economic stability in defusing traditional machismo: members of the "culture of poverty" value macho behavior, whereas Tzintzuntzan migrants, who have higher economic and social status, need not resort to overt public demonstrations of manhood.

6. Corwin (1963:37), among others, has remarked on a "cult of motherhood" in contemporary Mexico: "Nothing better illustrates the Motherhood Cult than Mother's Day itself, which like Christmas, has become a great commercial institution both in the United States and Mexico. But in Mexico the commercial facts are not so impressive as the overwhelming emotional fervor released on *el día de la madre*. The entire society seems to lift its eyes beyond the sad, proletarian image of helpless maternity to the idealized and undefiled, unselfish and disinterested."

CHAPTER 6

ECONOMIC ORGANIZATION

In the preceding chapter we described the structure and organization of Tzintzuntzan migrant families and households in Mexico City. Since many of the tensions affecting every migrant's daily routine derive from efforts to cope with pressing economic demands, analysis of the occupational situation is necessary. Subsequently we will describe how the relatively good economic statuses lead to living standards (as expressed through consumer behavior and housing quality) superior to that of the villagers in Tzintzuntzan and better than those of many natives of the capital.

For the 65 migrant households on which direct census data were obtained in 1974, 37% of the household heads are employed in "industrías de transformación" (such as steel and aluminum fabrication, automobile manufacture, chemicals, and plastics). Fifteen percent work in government jobs (especially as teachers). Fourteen percent work in commerce, and 11% are construction workers. In addition to these major categories, 9% of the migrant household heads are employed in the services sector and 5% work in transportation. Only 7% of the migrant households heads are not working, and 2% are in school. Seventy percent are "obreros" or "empleados;" only 15% work "por su cuenta." In sum, the migrants work in many occupational specialties—factory workers, teachers, civil servants, store clerks, soldiers, musicians, translators, pharmacists, and even computer analysts. Except for the few owners of small pottery resale stands, no migrants labor in specialties traditionally mastered in Tzintzuntzan.

Many households have more than one wage earner; in fact, for the 65 surveyed, only 34 (52.3%) have a single worker, while 19 (29.2%) have two, and another 12 (18.5%) have three or more, with a maximum of five reached in one house-

FIG. 6-1—This Tzintzuntzan migrant works as supervisor of computer operations for a government agency.

hold. Thus, during the period of my latest census (July-August 1974), a total of 113 persons were employed full-time, for an average of 1.74 per household. What is more striking is that so few persons were without work, even counting students and retirees. This high participation rate in the urban economy further demonstrates that these migrants indeed represent some of the best educated, most able, and most motivated members of their home community. It shows that peasants are not excluded from national economic development when their talents are utilized in the urban sector.

Despite the high number of households with more than a single worker, only a few contained individuals with two jobs. In each case, the jobs require similar skills (e.g., teaching) combined with relatively short hours for a single shift. For the great majority of Tzintzuntzeños in Mexico City, holding two full-time jobs is very difficult, since an average work-week lasts five and one-half or six days.

How can we account for the occupational distribution and high participation rate of these migrants? Since no relation appears to exist between skills learned in pottery-making, agriculture, or other traditional Tzintzuntzan occupations and jobs subsequently obtained in Mexico City, we must look elsewhere for an explanation. The "first job" is very important, because it gives these migrants an appreciation of their future prospects and difficulties. Most migrants come to the city without a job assured. Instead they hope to find work only after their arrival. Their hopes are based on the near-certainty that a friend or relative, already working in the capital, can expedite the job search. In addition to providing temporary lodging for recent arrivals, the more experienced migrants intercede as *"palancas"* or *"enchufes"* to obtain employment for new arrivals. The importance of the palanca, who serves as a mediator between rural and urban ways, is an extension of traditional patron-client ties found in Tzintzuntzan (cf. Foster 1967:241-242). The "senior" migrants receive social prestige (but not financial reward) in exchange for manipulating the real urban patrons—i.e., the supervisors and bosses who actually hand out jobs. Usually, the members of the household in which the new arrival lives upon reaching the city prove to be key resources.

The first urban job is usually a temporary commitment, especially since most Tzintzuntzeños, lacking appropriate experience or credentials for high-level occupations, enter the labor market in unskilled or semiskilled positions such as *albañil* or factory laborer. Recent government public works programs have lured a number of peasants to the capital. Tzintzuntzeños quickly master the skills required in most construction jobs; as the saying goes, *como el oficio del aguador—al primer viaje se aprende* ("like the water carrier's job, one learns it on the first trip"). Furthermore, as the following example demonstrates, when one migrant hears that more workers are needed on his construction job, he can quickly and inexpensively notify friends and relatives in the village about the opportunity.

In summer 1970 Armando Cornelio was an albañil in the public works construction project near the Aztec Stadium. When his boss asked for more workers, Armando returned to Tzintzuntzan that weekend and on Monday was joined by three other men, all of whom, like Armando, had left their wives and children in the village. All the men are potters, but since little pottery is produced in the summer rainy season, they look for outside work. In Mexico City, they will live in tents and shacks at the worksite until the construction is completed. Then, if they are rehired, they may continue to the next construction job with the same company; but if not rehired, they could either search for other temporary urban work or return to the village.

Whether working as albañiles or in some other job, new arrivals search for permanent employment by consulting

friends, relatives, compadres, fellow workers, and union officials. However, preference for utilizing personal networks
poses severe limitations on their urban job prospects, since
their opportunities are unlikely to be much superior to those
already occupied by members of their social networks. Nonetheless, as Simmons, Hanson, and Potter (1967:19) observe:

> Person to person communication about job oppor-
> tunities is certainly a traditional mode of search for
> rural people. . .and it is the most frequently successful
> mode of search in the city for unskilled workers.

Of course, the length of time necessary to find a "good"
job varies with the personal attributes the individual migrant
brings with him to the city and the sequence and quality of
his initial urban work and social experiences. Generally, Tzintzuntzeños find some work immediately upon arrival, but a
job good enough to really satisfy them seldom comes
quickly.

A few case histories will provide a better appreciation of
the complexity of the urban job search:

(1) Marcel Reyes first came to Mexico City at age 17 in
1967. He first worked as a grocery store stock-clerk for
a wage of 100 pesos a week, but lasted only 6 months.
Then, through the aid of a relative, he found work at a
bakery where he remained for 5 months at a salary of
150 pesos a week. He quit that job to work as a watchman and apprentice mechanic in a nearby garage, where
he took a pay cut to 100 pesos a week in exchange for
the chance to master a trade. When he failed to show
much aptitude for such work, he gave up on the urban
labor market temporarily, returned to Tzintzuntzan,
where he again worked as a pottery reseller and travelled
to the northern border region as a middleman. Although
profits were good, competition grew stiffer and profits

began to decline. So, he returned to the capital where he located work at a box-making factory where he earned the new minimum wage of 32 pesos a day. After four months, he managed to escape the drudgery of that occupation by passing an exam for bill collectors for a pharmaceutical firm. This was his best job to date, and he earned 70 pesos a day in wages and commissions. Unfortunately, his lack of a primary school diploma prevented him from being immediately rehired after the six-month probationary contract had terminated, so while he awaited a decision concerning his chances there, he began looking for other employment possibilities. Through Emiliano Guzmán he got work at a metals factory as a common laborer, and has remained there because the pharmaceutical firm never renewed his contract. Since his brother is unable to work until litigation over an industrial accident is completed and the medical benefits paid, Marcel is presently supporting his widowed mother (who does a little washing and ironing each day to earn perhaps 100 pesos a week) and his three younger siblings living in the family's one-room plus kitchen apartment for which the rent is 200 pesos a month.

(2) Gilberto Correa, age 26, is a Sergeant in the Mexican Army and has been stationed in Sinaloa, Jalisco, Michoacán, and Mexico City during his eight-year career. Currently, he is in the capital where he attends the Colegio Militar half-time for further training in his special field of arms repair. He has encouraged other villagers to join the Army because of its good pay and benefits, but so far only two have joined him—and both have the same specialty as Gilberto. They all earn more than 1,000 pesos a month plus various allowances and military allotments. Gilberto and the others normally work a five-day week and find the Army a congenial

career with opportunity for advancement in their specialties. Gilberto told Raúl Silva about the opportunities, but Raúl proved to be too short to pass the physical examination, besides not being especially enthusiastic about military life despite his friend's encouragement.

(3) Unlike many migrants, Fernando Cuevas has had but two principal jobs during a decade in Mexico City. The first, as a night watchman, was arranged through a nephew who recommended Fernando to the priest in Quiroga, who in turn knew the priest in charge of a church school in Mexico City where Fernando was taken on. The second job, which he has had for several years, is as an albañil, a position Fernando likes because it is outdoors rather than inside work, and was arranged through an engineer who had accepted an offer of *compadrazgo de bautismo* for one of Fernando's sons. Once linked as compadres, Fernando used the engineer as a palanca to attain a job.

(4) Leonel Castillo, first arrived in Mexico City in 1936, where he lived with an older brother and worked as a peón at the same factory. After a few years, he took an interest in truck driving, earned his license, and has since been a well-paid driver. He stayed with the same company for years but tired of the routine; eager to learn more about the United States and the northern border region, he joined, for a five-year period (1958 to 1963), the Mexican Army where he served as a Sergeant and truckdriver. In 1964 he returned to the city, found that his old boss had moved to another company, joined him there as a driver with de planta status; and he has since arranged for his 17-year-old son, as well as three other migrants, to be hired on as laborers at the metals firm.

In contrast to their initial employment instability, most Tzintzuntzeños in the capital soon settle into permanent occupational niches, with which they are generally satisfied. This does not mean that workers retain the same job year after year; on the contrary, they continually search for better occupational opportunities, with the final decision to change careers or company affiliations determined by three main factors: wages, tenure, and social security benefits.

While wages are important, their virtual uniformity throughout the city for specific work categories (because of government wage-and-price controls) makes tenure a principal goal for workers who have been laboring on short-term (one- to six-month) contracts. When a worker is *de planta*, he feels that he is no longer a humble *obrero* but is instead an *empleado de confianza*. He has simultaneously won his employer's trust and has gained benefits reserved to tenured personnel (e.g., vacations, sick-leave, holidays, and better medical and social security coverage).

Most Tzintzuntzan migrants in Mexico City are satisfied with their current employment more from a perceptive appreciation of their own abilities and prospects in the urban economy than from a lack of desire to improve themselves further. Few dream of becoming wealthy, but some hope to shift from manual labor to "professional" status, and most believe that their children will enter the ranks of white-collar workers. Therefore, most workers hope to acquire tenure in their present line of work in order to gain more seniority and higher income rather than risk temporary unemployment while searching for a better job. This basically conservative attitude toward their participation in the urban job market is reflected by responses to the question, "If you could choose any job you wanted, what would you choose?" Nearly every informant explicitly took into account his present skills and education. One worker aptly summed up the prevailing attitude: "I would like to be an office worker, because it is cleaner and less physically taxing, but I don't think I am qualified because of my lack of schooling." Another responded: "I would work in my same line of work (i.e., as a factory laborer) but desire something as secure as possible."

What is striking about Tzintzuntzan migrant attitudes toward the possibility of upward economic mobility is their acute awareness of the difficulties for improving oneself without adequate job experience and educational preparation in the overcrowded urban job marketplace. The migrants are content to earn wages sufficient for the basic needs of their families, since such wages far exceed their equivalents in Tzintzuntzan. In other words, the workers' sense of satisfaction and self-esteem derived from urban jobs is assessed according to rural as well as urban standards of success. Tzintzuntzan migrants in Mexico City generally compare their present situation with that of their fathers and their siblings still in the village, and most believe that the urban condition is far superior. Few migrants view their progress according to the same middle-class standard that most social scientists employ when assessing mobility and aspirations. Those who do tend to isolate themselves from the rest of the Tzintzuntzeños in the city as they shift their allegiance from rural and lower-class standards of success to urban and middle-class models of achievement.

The shift from rural to urban concepts of economic status forms an integral part of the assimilation process undergone by the Tzintzuntzan migrants in Mexico City. One indication that even working-class migrants eventually become more sophisticated in understanding the demands of the urban economy is that whereas nearly all got their first urban jobs through personal networks of friends and relatives, more experienced workers prefer to consult non-Tzintzuntzeño allies, especially superiors on the job, friends in the unions, or government bureaucrats who might become more useful palancas. Another indication of changing attitudes among longer-term urban residents is that none would consider returning to Tzintzuntzan as an alternative to seeking other

urban employment if they lost their present jobs. Thus, Tzintzuntzeños in Mexico City eventually realize that while fellow migrants can assist one to locate initial urban employment, subsequent upward mobility is more often the result of
individual initiative and hard work. As one informant remarked, "If a good job exists, then only a fool would pass it
up and give it to his *paisano*."

The independence and isolation of the few Tzintzuntzeños
who already have succeeded to the point of attaining middle-
class status is hardly surprising in the light of such attitudes.
Upward occupational mobility means not only shifting one's
allegiance to a new set of achievement models but also results
in sloughing off a sense of commonality with those who fail
to match those achievements. The rift between "los inferiores" and "los superiores," as one middle-class informant
expressed it, duplicates the incipient class distinctions now
found in the village but with a further consequence: the urban setting provides much greater opportunity for widening
the gap between the poor and the affluent. It remains to be
seen whether the recently established migrant association can
close the gap.

ENTREPRENEURIAL ACTIVITY

Few Tzintzuntzan migrants are self-employed within the
urban economy. Although a small number operate stands for
the sale of crafts near the famous church in Los Remedios,
on the western edge of the city, nearly all adults depend on
jobs in factories or with the government to support their
families. This seems to be a predominant aspect of the early
phases of urban adaptation. After spending some years in the
city, however, during which time familiarity with urban
entrepreneurial opportunity increases, it appears that some
migrants are willing to risk going into business for themselves.
This is especially the case for those who are aware that they

have reached the limit of their job ability to propel their families up the socioeconomic ladder.

Entrepreneurial activities among the migrants take several forms. Particularly popular is the reselling of pottery, crafts, and agricultural products brought to the capital after visits to the village. A sufficient profit can be made through these small-scale transactions, usually through sales to neighbors and work companions, to pay for the trip back to Tzintzuntzan. An extension of this reselling role is their involvement in buying U.S.-produced goods and bringing them back to Mexico City for profitable resale. This sort of reselling often places the migrants into jeopardy for dealing in contraband. A final form of entrepreneurship is the establishment of a family business, especially a small store which can be staffed by different family members throughout the week. Several migrant families have expressed interest in opening small stores, but most currently lack the necessary start-up capital and the appropriate manpower within the family unit.

It seems likely that the emergence of family firms as a significant mechanism of urban economic adaptation among the Tzintzuntzan migrants can occur only at certain points in the family domestic cycle. A family needs two or more children between 15 and 25 years of age who are not otherwise employed in a more profitable activity. Recently married children can, of course, bring their new spouses into the family business as an additional employee. It remains to be seen if the model of entrepreneurial success displayed in the example of the Rodolfo Campos family will be emulated by other Tzintzuntzan migrants and their children. A fortunate combination of events, beginning with a nephew's part-time job in a liquor-grocery store and ending with Rodolfo's buying out its owner, turned the Campos family into entrepreneurs. From that initial step in 1973, which involved a down payment of only a few thousand pesos, the family's business activities have expanded to include a school supplies store and an auto parts and service store.

FIG. 6-2—The Campos family took over this small liquor-grocery store in 1973 and have worked 14 hours a day, 7 days a week in their efforts to make a good profit.

FIG. 6-3—The Campos family opened this small school supplies store in 1974. It is located in the front of a relative's house, across the street from a new school complex.

FIG. 6-4—The third Campos family business, an auto parts and service operation, opened in 1976 next door to their school supplies store. Each of the family's three adult children, a nephew, and two spouses contribute to these family firms and earn profits from them.

INCOME AND CONSUMER BEHAVIOR

Stability of urban occupation encourages adoption of consumer behavior patterns unworkable within the framework of traditional village life. The principal difference between urban and traditional rural occupations is the degree of dependence on cash income. Villagers usually keep gardens, fruit trees, and domestic animals to supplement the cash income from pottery-making, farming, and other traditional occupations. Tzintzuntzeño families in Mexico City are completely subject to the vagaries of the cash nexus. In the migrant households for which I have detailed economic data, productive gardens and fruit trees are completely absent and domestic animals are present in only a few, with none having more than four chickens or a single pig. Of course, the absence of such supplements to cash income could be due more to the lack of space in crowded homes than to changing attitudes of most migrants in Mexico City.

Migrant income levels vary with type of profession, number of workers per household, and number of jobs which each worker holds. For instance, in one household five men are employed; and although none earns much more than 300 pesos per week, the total household income is about 1,500 pesos per week. By contrast, one household head works as a teacher in a private elementary school each morning, then serves as a public school principal each afternoon in order to earn 950 pesos a week altogether. And another man who works as a translator for an American company earns some 9,000 pesos per month between salary and extra compensations.

Table 6-1 gives the household income distribution for Tzintzuntzeños in Mexico City during 1974. Most workers earn the minimum wage or more and work at full-time jobs. In comparison with the general urban income distribution, it

TABLE 6-1
Household Income Level for
Tzintzuntzan Migrants in Mexico City—1974

Weekly Income Level	Number	Percent
0–249 pesos	1	1.5
250–499 pesos	31	47.7
500–749 pesos	10	15.4
750–999 pesos	3	4.6
1,000–1,499 pesos	9	13.8
1,500–1,999 pesos	2	3.1
2,000+ pesos	4	6.2
Missing data	5	7.7
Total	65	100.0

Note: No household has a total weekly income higher than 3,000 pesos per week.

is obvious that the great majority of Tzintzuntzan migrants in Mexico City belong to the working or middle classes, with none at the poorest level and only a few well-off.

Migrants are well aware that their jobs provide the basis for urban livelihood and so learn to adjust residence patterns, social relations, and child-raising practices to the demands of the city. It is notable that children, especially, are expected to devote their time and attention to school work rather than to become involved in activities like selling *chicles* or newspapers in the streets—parents correctly comprehend that these activities bring little return on the investment of their children's time and energy. Thus, urban job requirements and parental attitudes reverse the traditional view of the economic struggle found in most Tzintzuntzan families, where

> A living . . . is earned by nearly everyone in bits and pieces. Every family member is alert to the possibility of picking up a few extra pesos here and there, and rare is a person who, in addition to his primary occupation, does not try his hand at other tasks (Foster 1967:47).

Despite much higher income levels than they would enjoy in Tzintzuntzan, the migrant families must struggle with elevated prices for consumer goods and services. Whereas few persons earn more than 100 pesos a week in Tzintzuntzan, families in the capital require at least 300 pesos a week to eke out a minimal urban living standard.

Based on detailed budgetary data for a few households and census data for the rest, I believe that most Tzintzuntzeños in Mexico City spend nearly all of their incomes on basic food, clothing, and housing costs, with the percentages varying somewhat between poorer and more affluent families. The poorest migrants spend about 50% of their limited incomes on food, 20% on housing, and 20% on clothing, so that little remains for the purchase of major consumer goods. In contrast, middle-class families spend only 20% to 30% of their higher incomes on food, 15% on housing, and 20% to 30% on clothing. This leaves a substantial surplus for buying television sets, refrigerators, stoves, and other expensive consumer goods. Thus, the essential difference between the poorest and most affluent Tzintzuntzeños in the city is the frequency with which such "luxuries" can be purchased. Steady income permits urban survival; higher income allows migrants to incorporate into the daily budget consumer goods that permit a living standard far beyond that enjoyed by most Tzintzuntzan villagers.

The relation between income and consumer behavior can also be examined through analysis of the distribution of major material possessions. In comparison with village households, the migrant households in the capital own more consumer goods, with differences for specific items ranging from an average of 30% to as high as 80%. A basic distinction between rural and urban buying patterns is reflected in attitudes toward sleeping arrangements: the traditional *petate* is absent in migrant households and is replaced by store-bought mattresses, frames, and bedding, with the ideal arrangement providing separate beds for each child and a large double bed for the parents.

The transformation in sleeping arrangements has a double significance. First, the typical migrant household contains several beds, nearly always purchased with cash rather than on credit. Second, giving children their own beds sharply contrasts with traditional village practice wherein children are expected to share a common petate or bed at least through adolescence. Thus, modification of sleeping arrangements illustrates another way in which migrants discard traditional behavior even though extra expenditure is required. As an extension of these changes, elaborate bedroom furniture becomes an important indicator of economic and social standing. More affluent families spend thousands of pesos for complete bedroom sets—consisting of double bed, dresser with mirror, wardrobe chest, and end tables—in order to validate their toehold in, and affiliation with, a lifestyle distinct from that in which they were reared in Tzintzuntzan and that in which poorer urban families still participate. Of course, the bed is an important symbol even in the poorest households; in fact, it assumes predominance by serving as the focal point of nearly all activities—as sleeping area, couch, playpen, and work area—since it is often the principal piece of furniture in otherwise ill-equipped slum apartments (cf. Lewis 1969: 117-118).

In addition to bedroom furniture, all migrant households contain at least a table, chairs, wardrobe closets, and dish shelves. After these ubiquitous necessities—radios (94%), electric irons (80%), televisions (75%), propane stoves (72%), and electric blenders (58%)—are found in the majority of migrant homes. Stereo consoles or record players (46%), sewing machines (29%), refrigerators (20%), automatic washing machines (20%), automobiles (14%), and telephones (3%) are less common and generally are restricted to the more affluent homes.

Curiously, ownership of a refrigerator does not significantly alter the usual daily buying patterns. All families prefer fresh produce, meats, and dairy products rather than the more expensive, less flavorful and beneficial—to use the migrants' terms—frozen equivalents. Refrigerators more often hold beer and soft drinks than foods bought in anticipation of future needs.

With respect to buying habits, most migrants prefer to purchase consumer goods for cash rather than on credit. As the saying goes, *No quiero endrogarme* ("I don't like to fall into debt"—literally, "get drugged"). Credit is sought primarily for buying television sets, automobiles and similar very expensive items. Some families try to put aside a small amount of money out of each paycheck toward future purchases rather than to pay high interest rates for installment purchases. Nevertheless, in spite of general attitudes about the use of credit, it is a rare family that is not seduced by the easy availability of credit for consumer goods.

HOUSING QUALITY AND LIVING STANDARDS

In addition to fundamental transformations in their income and consumer behavior, Tzintzuntzan migrants in the capital usually inhabit dwellings with more comforts and conveniences than their village counterparts enjoy. All of the migrant households have electricity; 85% have *drenaje*, and 77% have direct access to water, either in their kitchens or in a patio water tap. Sixty-nine percent have glass windows, and 60% have painted or whitewashed facades. Forty-nine percent have three or more rooms. Single-room apartments are found among only 14% of the migrants and two-room places among 35%. Three-room residences are found among 15%; the largest homes (5%) have nine rooms. In addition, 43% of the homes have private bathroom facilities, and 22% have shower baths also. Only 6% of the homes have earthen floors.

Most migrants live in small, rented apartments, while only a minority (31%) own homes or are currently paying off home mortgages. The goal to which all migrants aspire is ownership of their own home, with several bedrooms, indoor plumbing, patio or yard, and running water. Only a few households have all of these characteristics today, but achieving these living conditions appears to be a major motivation for trying to get ahead in the city.

Tzintzuntzeños particularly dislike the lack of privacy and sense of independence which they associate with cramped urban apartments. On the one hand, they recall the relative spaciousness of the homes (including patios) they grew up in; and, on the other, they admire the luxuriousness of upperclass homes, whose grounds are surrounded by high walls topped by broken glass and barbed wire. Thus, a concern with privacy is neither an urban or rural preoccupation but, rather, pervades the city as well as the countryside; unfortunately, to recreate rural open space in the city requires much greater wealth than Tzintzuntzan migrants possess, so the only alternative lies in moving out of the maelstrom of the inner city. Of course, this does not convey the same meaning to poor and affluent families: the former look for a small plot of marginal land on the urban periphery, whereas the latter search for a subdivision in the suburbs where uniform building codes and appropriate middle- and upper-class standards are maintained through payment of high, long-term mortgages. In both instances, however, escaping the feeling of social claustrophobia of the urban sprawl is the main impetus to this centrifugal movement.

Regardless of aspirations, Tzintzuntzeños in Mexico City currently possess better quality housing and more consumer goods than do persons who remained in the village. To compare the two groups, I modified the Standard of Living Index used in Chapter 2 by replacing "raised hearth" (worth 2 points), an item absent in the city, with "refrigerator" and "telephone" (each worth 1 point). The differences in overall living standards between the village and migrant households are striking. No migrant household had a score below seven in 1970, and the mean score for migrants (17.7) was measurably higher than that in Tzintzuntzan (10.8). More specifically, rural-urban comparisons reveal that, whereas none of the migrant households had scores below seven, 29.9% of the village households were in this range; the 7-14 category included 33.4% of migrant households vs. 40.3% of the village households; the 15-24 group reversed the ratio—45.2% vs. 27.6%. The contrast at the top of the scale is also striking: 21.6% of migrant households were between 25-30 vs. a mere 2.2% for village households. The relatively higher scores on the Standard of Living Index show quite clearly that despite some complaints about lack of space in urban residences, migrants, as a group, experience major improvements in living standards after migration. Naturally, such obvious economic prosperity vis-à-vis Tzintzuntzan villagers constantly reinforces the validity of the original decision to emigrate.

While statistical evidence of high living standards among the migrant population is irrefutable, examination of particular cases better provides an appreciation of the actual range of housing quality and material possessions that constitute a specific score on the Index. For this reason, in Table 6-2 I present detailed information for three migrant households. The range of material possessions found in these three households is evidence of the importance which high income and length of urban residence play in the standard of living of specific families. It also illustrates the degree to which the poor families differ from their more affluent fellow migrants than from their rural counterparts.

It is not surprising that Tzintzuntzeños in Mexico City also compare their lot with other urbanites as well as with residents of the home community: in the process they abhor the consequences of urban poverty and admire the affluence of *la genta buena*. Of course, no migrant family can be placed properly at either end of that continuum, for none fit the multifarious characteristics (one is tempted to say, nefarious) of the members of the "culture of poverty" as Lewis has described the residents of the vecindad slums of the *herradura de tugurios* ("horseshoe-shaped zone of slums") in central Mexico City, nor do they qualify for membership in the elite segment of society which earns income from rents, investments, and the labor of others.

Although we can readily appreciate why the Tzintzuntzeños in the capital should not (at least, yet) pertain to the elite, an examination of why they are essentially outside of the "culture of poverty" is noteworthy. In a detailed compilation of "The Possessions of the Poor," Lewis (1969:114-124) outlined the results of his fieldwork in a poor tenement building in Mexico City. He found that "substantial proportions of the people's possessions had been bought secondhand" (1969:115); that "the tenants' principal possession was furniture, accounting for about a third of all their expenditures on material goods" (1969:116-117); that "in most households some members (usually the older sons) had to sleep on straw mats or rags on the floor" (1969:117); and went on to conclude that "brevity

TABLE 6-2

Household Inventory for Three Tzintzuntzan Migrant Families in Mexico City—1970

Item[a] Index Score	Household No. 1 13	Household No. 2 21	Household No. 3 27
Rent/month	150 pesos	0 (home paid for)	285 pesos (subsidized)
No. of Rooms	1	5	5
Floor Type	Earth	Concrete	Cement/linoleum
Wall Type	Scrap lumber	Concrete block	Block/stucco
Roof Type	Lumber/tarpaper	Corrugated sheetrock	Block/plaster
Electricity	1 Light bulb	Outlets in each room	Outlets in each room
Water Access	Shared (patio)	Private (patio)	Private (indoor)
Sewer Access	Tube (patio)	Underground (patio)	Indoor plumbing
Toilet Type	Shared latrine	W.C. room in patio	Indoor W.C.
Bathroom	No shower/bath	Shower (wood fire)	Shower/bath (hot water)
Patio	Dirt yard (share)	Cement (private)	No (3rd fl. apt.)
Possessions			
Beds	2 [bought secondhand]	4 [bought new]	3 [bought new]
Sofa	None	W/ 2 side chairs	W/ 2 side chairs
Stove	Propane	Propane	Propane
Radio	Transistor	2 (1 transistor & stereo console)	Stereo console
Television	None	None	B/W table model

TABLE 6-2 (Cont.)

Refrigerator	None	None	W/freezer
Electric Iron	1	1 plus 2 non-electric	3
Electric Blender	None	1	2
Sewing Machine	None	None	1
Automatic Washing Machine	None	None	1
Heater	None	Wood-burner, for water;	Gas-type
Telephone	None	None	None
Automobile	None	Motorcycle	None
Encyclopedia	None	None	Yes
Servant	None	None	Woman, live-in
Dining Set/Chairs	Wood table, 1 wood chair	Formica set w/4 chairs	Carved wooden for six
Cabinet for Dishes	Shelf on wall	Metal shelf (glass-enclosed)	Elaborate, carved breakfront
Dishes/Glassware Sets	Miscl. unmatched pieces	Set of smoked glassware	Set of Tzintzuntzan pottery
Bedroom Furniture Sets	None; only bed and unmatched wardrobe	None; 2 wardrobes, dresser w/ mirror--not matched to beds	2 complete furniture sets
Animals	None	2 songbirds and 2 dogs	None
Plants	None	Flowers in pots on patio	Plastic flowers atop stereo

[a]Naturally, only the most important items are listed in this Table; also, I have specifically excluded clothing, but this also increases in quantity and quality from Household No. 1 through Household No. 3.

of possession, and the singular absence of heirlooms passed down from generation to generation, suggest that the life of the very poor is weak in tradition and is oriented almost exclusively to day-to-day concerns" (1969:124).

In contrast, only the poorest Tzintzuntzan migrants, such as Household No. 1 in Table 6-2, purchase any goods secondhand—all prefer to buy goods new whenever possible. Furniture per se ceases to be the most important possession as affluence outstrips the available space in apartments and homes, and no one among the Tzintzuntzeños in Mexico City sleeps on petates on the floor.

Whether the lives of Tzintzuntzan migrant families are weak in tradition is a debatable point, since, on the one hand, the length of time during which most have been in Mexico City is less than a generation and on the other hand "tradition" is usually thought of in reference to rural ways discarded or devalued by the very act of emigration. Nevertheless, it seems certain that few Tzintzuntzan migrants can be expected to fall into the cyclical, self-perpetuating system of affairs which supposedly characterizes the "culture of poverty."

The Tzintzuntzan migrants have a strong orientation toward the future. Their long-term economic struggles, as evidenced in the initial job search, later occupational stability, and consequent improvement in housing quality and overall living standards, provide uncontestable evidence to them that the road to ultimate prosperity is not closed. Poverty is a condition to be overcome. The first step came when they left the village and the second when they gained steady urban employment. The third, but perhaps penultimate step, occurs as their children learn urban ways as expressed in educational standards, consumer attitudes, transformation of worldview, and achievement of upward mobility. So far, no aspirations have been crushed by external, uncontrollable forces, such as an economic depression or increased competition for urban employment. If this should occur, then frustration, anger, and sadness might replace the people's rising expectations. Few Tzintzuntzan migrants are pessimistic. Most would agree with the informant who remarked,

> "What are my dreams? Well, with hard work a person begins to think about his future, in having his own home, in helping his children and in seeing them achieve a social and economic level that he himself doesn't enjoy."

SUMMARY

The Tzintzuntzan migrants have an exceptional participation in the urban economy, especially in the industrial and governmental services sectors. The use of palancas to assist fellow migrants in finding employment, particularly a first job, is widespread among the migrants, as it is among Mexican workers in general. In the job search, there is a potential conflict between the desire for job security and the desire for upward mobility. Few migrants expect to become wealthy, but many hope to provide a base from which their children can eventually progress. The recognition of the importance of job experience and educational preparation is a crucial part of the Tzintzuntzeño success in the urban marketplace. Although workers earn the minimum wage or only slightly more, some earn excellent incomes which place them in the middle class of urban Mexican society. As a result, the migrants generally enjoy a satisfying standard of living, although many are unhappy with the cramped quarters they inhabit until they are able to purchase their own lot and house. This appears to be a primary goal of the migrants' economic endeavors in the urban setting.

CHAPTER 7

SOCIAL ORGANIZATION

Migration to Mexico City thrusts Tzintzuntzeños into a new world of social relations. The two great categories of peasant life—"villagers" vs. "outsiders"—are ultimately obliterated through participation in city life. Kinship and friendship ties are expanded beyond the migrant group in the efforts of emigrants to better manipulate urban resources. And urban geographical distances and class differences modify traditional attitudes toward social interaction.

When Tzintzuntzan peasants arrive in the city they usually depend on their fellow ex-villagers to locate work and housing for them. Subsequently, new arrivals meet other city residents on the job and in the neighborhood and so cease to be encapsulated by fellow migrants. This expansion in reference group from fellow migrants to include other urban residents is a critical phase in urban adaptation, since upward social and economic mobility is often related to involvement with non-Tzintzuntzeños in Mexico City.

SOCIAL INTERACTION AND SOCIAL NETWORKS

As a consequence of the pressures exerted by urban geography and because of traditional patterns of social relations, Tzintzuntzeños in the capital prefer to base their social ties upon a series of overlapping ego-centered social networks. Individual social contacts tend to be concentrated in the primary family group and within local enclaves. Participation in formal organizations is limited to membership in unions or professional organizations related to one's occupational speciality; neighborhood and other voluntary associations, including political parties, appear to be of little importance.

No formal or informal association of Tzintzuntzan migrants existed in Mexico City until the summer of 1975, although a basketball team flourished briefly among some young migrants in 1974. Absence of such a voluntary association provides an important clue to understanding the migrants' participation in the urban social world: first, it means that social integration among the migrants has rested solely on kinship, friendship, or *compadrazgo* ties, often established prior to migration; second, limiting social relations among migrants has encouraged an outward search for potential urban contacts; finally, urban adaptation has depended on a pragmatic analysis of one's social options rather than on an extension of initial dependence on those migrants with greater exposure to the city. If the new migrant association is successful, perhaps it will provide a forum for these social relationships.[1]

FIG. 7-1—Several young migrants formed a basketball team in 1974.

Social relations among Tzintzuntzeños in the capital are based on dyadic contacts in which mutual expectations and obligations exist within a system of reciprocal, multi-purpose ties. This is particularly significant since urban geographical separation permits migrants to choose relatives and friends with whom social interaction is desirable and ignore those with whom reciprocal relations are unwanted.

Dyadic social relations provide Tzintzuntzan migrants with sufficient emotional and economic stability so that urban adaptation proceeds without "breakdown." Tzintzuntzeños do not fit the category of "marginal" migrants unwilling or unable to participate fully in the urban social system. On the contrary, the relative weakness of social ties *within* the migrant population emphasizes the stability and strength of the migrant family and permits easy expansion of personal social networks into other sectors of urban culture.

To paraphrase Germani (1967:179), the maintenance of strong ties with fellow migrants may ease the initial *adjustment* of new arrivals in the city but need not facilitate their *assimilation* to the urban culture. In other words, the transference of rural values, expectations, and obligations in urban social relations is not homologous with assimilation of urban patterns of social behavior, especially where significant differences in village and city patterns are present. Social integration among migrants that depends on the persistence of rural models of behavior can be counter-productive of effective participation in urban social systems and lead instead to "marginality."

Under these urban conditions, I found that the insights of social network analysis proved particularly helpful in understanding the totality of migrant social relations without losing sight of the significant differences which exist among individual Tzintzuntzeños in Mexico City. Furthermore, examination of personal networks, based on reciprocal dyadic contracts, shows how Tzintzuntzeños shift from a restricted view of the urban social system to a broadly-based

FIG. 7-2–The banner of the migrant association at the Campos home.
It goes from house to house on a rotating monthly basis.

participation in social alliances related to occupational and
eventually neighborhood commitments. Thus, the "urbanization" of migrant social relations–i.e., the shift from dependence on fellow migrants to a search for ties with other, often
more powerful, urban allies–is crucial to their strategies for
upward socioeconomic mobility.

In an effort to measure the degree and type of social interaction among Tzintzuntzan migrants in Mexico City, I asked
a heterogeneous sample of 39 adults, living in 25 households,
to report on their relations with 141 other adult migrants
between July 1969 and July 1970. (Subsequent census analysis showed that 160 adult Tzintzuntzeños lived in Mexico
City during some part of this period. However, I believe that
the sample included here is still representative enough for
analytical purposes.)

Table 7-1 lists migrant responses according to type of relationship and Table 7-2 gives the frequency of migrant visits.

TABLE 7-1
Social Relations among Tzintzuntzan Migrants

Respondents Individual	Household*	Not Know	Knows	Friend	Relative	Compadre
1	R	110	18	2	11	0
2	A	50	28	56	7	0
3	C	116	12	5	8	0
4	B	90	34	5	10	1
5	C	54	64	10	11	2
6	C	107	16	10	8	0
7	I	117	12	6	6	0
8	D	125	44	3	8	1
9	Q	47	86	3	4	1
10	E	85	45	5	6	0
11	F	13	114	4	7	3
12	G	127	13	0	1	0
13	G	132	2	6	1	0
14	H	42	94	0	5	0
15	A	103	19	7	10	2
16	E	53	73	5	9	1
17	E	16	116	1	8	0
18	S	99	38	1	3	0
19	I	129	8	1	2	1
20	J	24	109	1	7	0
21	H	36	84	13	8	0
22	X	60	70	0	11	0
23	U	139	1	0	1	0
24	W	37	101	0	3	0
25	Y	75	64	0	1	1
26	V	50	86	0	5	0
27	P	75	44	5	14	2
28	J	33	105	2	1	0
29	J	50	86	3	2	0
30	K	47	64	22	8	0
31	K	64	62	11	4	0
32	T	74	44	13	10	0
33	K	113	12	4	11	1
34	L	95	35	2	8	1
35	B	62	58	4	15	2
36	M	82	52	0	7	0
37	N	82	54	0	5	0
38	O	71	57	8	3	2
39	F	29	100	0	11	1
	Mean	74.7	53.4	5.6	6.7	0.6
	Ranges					
	Low	13	1	0	1	0
	High	139	116	56	15	3

*See Fig. 4-1.

TABLE 7-2
Visiting Patterns among Tzintzuntzan Migrants

Respondents Individual	Household*	None	Seldom (1-6/yr)	Frequent (7-24/yr)	Regular (25+/yr)	Live With
1	R	137	4	0	0	0
2	A	134	2	4	0	1
3	C	123	12	4	0	2
4	B	121	15	0	4	1
5	C	124	10	2	3	2
6	C	122	7	6	4	2
7	I	133	6	0	2	0
8	D	130	9	1	1	0
9	Q	134	2	1	4	0
10	E	130	8	1	0	2
11	F	121	17	0	2	1
12	G	138	2	0	0	1
13	G	132	8	0	0	1
14	H	121	10	8	0	2
15	A	133	7	0	0	1
16	E	128	5	0	6	2
17	E	132	6	0	0	3
18	S	137	1	0	2	1
19	I	137	2	0	2	0
20	J	126	11	0	2	2
21	H	134	5	0	0	2
22	X	136	2	0	2	1
23	U	139	0	0	1	1
24	W	136	5	0	0	0
25	Y	140	0	0	1	0
26	V	136	3	0	1	1
27	P	133	6	2	0	0
28	J	107	31	0	2	1
29	J	128	9	0	2	2
30	K	117	21	1	0	2
31	K	127	5	3	4	2
32	T	138	2	1	0	0
33	K	131	7	1	0	2
34	L	137	2	1	0	1
35	B	123	12	2	3	1
36	M	137	1	0	1	2
37	N	137	1	0	3	0
38	O	133	7	1	0	0
39	F	134	3	0	3	1
	Mean	130.6	6.9	1.0	1.4	1.1
	Ranges					
	Low	107	0	0	0	0
	High	140	31	8	6	3

*See Fig. 4-1.

Even a cursory examination of these tables demonstrates that knowledge of other migrants varies tremendously and that friendship, kinship, and compadrazgo ties are infrequent. If the statistical mean score represents a "typical" migrant, then such an individual would know (i.e., recognize the name of, in most cases) some 53 other migrants, would be related to seven, be friends with another six, and perhaps be *compadre* of one more. Analysis of migrant visiting patterns shows that a "typical" migrant would have visited or been visited by only nine migrants outside his immediate household and would have seen only two or three fellow migrants frequently or regularly.

To proceed from a collection of personal networks to a description of the "total network" of Tzintzuntzan migrants in Mexico City would require that every migrant be queried on his social relations with all others. Since this proved impracticable in the field, I shall limit my discussion to those 25 migrant households in which the 39 respondents lived at the time of the interviews. I combined these personal links into "household networks" in order to gain a clearer perspective on migrant social relations.

When Tzintzuntzan migrants see each other in Mexico City, this almost always occurs in one of their homes. Nevertheless, the migrants consider their relationships to be individualistic and not binding on other family members. Thus, my analysis of households represents a second-level abstraction from social reality. This approach is justified because the conceptual problems of dealing with a 39 x 39 matrix are reduced and because my data on socioeconomic status and related parameters are derived from household census schedules.

Although the network approach utilized here relies on analysis of relatively short-term social ties, I want to emphasize that I do not conceive of migrant social relations as in any way forming a static pattern. As Gulliver (1971:352) has cautioned, this procedure of lifting "something like *the* social network. . .out of the continuum of social life by analytical procedures and for analytical convenience. . .introduces a danger that needs to be recognized and guarded against." But in the absence of any association or community units of analysis the social network approach gives a good heuristic approximation of Tzintzuntzeño social adaptation to life in Mexico City.

Table 7-3 is a matrix of visiting patterns among 25 Tzintzuntzan migrant households for the period between July 1969 and June 1970. I have followed Gulliver's (1971:279) suggestion that visiting is "a good indication of an active relationship." Only 64 links of a theoretical maximum of 300 (i.e., n[n-1]/2, where n = 25) were active during this period. And only 15 of these involved "strong" ties, which I have operationally defined as more than 6 visits in 12 months. The average number of different households visited was only five, and only 24% of the households maintained strong ties with another household. At one extreme, household "Y" had no links with any other households; at the other extreme, household "B" had ties with 13 others.

Active social relations between these migrant households depend on status homogeneity, not status heterogeneity. That is, households of similar socioeconomic status and similar lengths of urban residence are more likely to maintain social ties, especially strong links, than are households in dissimilar categories. Even the *arrimado* and *palanca* mechanisms for initial social adjustment to city life do not truly violate this principle; they occur among persons who define themselves as *relative* equals. Middle-class migrants assist relatively affluent villagers, while working-class migrants help poorer villagers.

Status homogeneity, defined in terms of income levels and living standards, explains 67% (10 of 15) of the strong ties, and 57% (28 of 49) of the weak ties between the migrant households surveyed. When defined in terms of length of urban residence, status homogeneity explains 67% of the

TABLE 7-3

Visiting Patterns among Migrant Households

	A	B	C	D	E	F	G	H	I	J	K	L	M	N	O	P	Q	R	S	T	U	V	W	X	Y	Total
A	–	w	s	w	–	–	w	–	–	–	w	–	w	–	–	–	–	w	w	–	–	–	w	–	–	7
B		–	s	w	w	w	w	s	w	w	w	w	w	w	w	–	w	w	w	–	–	w	–	w	–	12
C			–	–	s	w	–	w	w	s	w	–	w	–	w	–	w	s	–	s	–	–	–	–	–	5
D				–	–	w	–	–	–	w	–	–	w	–	–	w	–	–	–	–	–	–	–	–	–	5
E					–	w	w	–	s	–	w	–	w	w	–	s	–	w	w	–	–	w	w	–	–	7
F						–	–	s	–	w	s	–	s	s	w	–	w	w	–	–	w	w	–	–	–	7
G							–	–	–	–	–	w	–	–	–	–	–	–	–	–	–	–	–	–	–	1
H								–	–	–	w	–	–	–	w	–	–	–	–	–	–	–	–	s	–	2
I									–	w	w	–	–	w	–	–	w	–	w	–	w	–	–	–	–	3
J										–	w	–	–	–	w	–	–	–	–	–	–	–	w	w	–	4
K											–	w	–	–	w	–	–	–	–	–	–	–	–	–	–	2
L												–	–	–	–	–	–	–	–	–	–	–	–	–	–	0
M													–	s	w	w	–	–	–	–	–	–	–	w	–	2
N														–	–	–	w	–	–	–	–	–	–	–	–	1
O															–	–	–	–	–	–	–	–	w	–	–	1
P																–	–	–	–	–	–	–	–	–	–	0
Q																	–	w	–	–	–	–	–	–	–	0
R																		–	–	–	–	–	–	–	–	0
S																			–	–	s	w	w	–	–	2
T																				–	–	–	–	s	–	2
U																					–	–	–	w	–	1
V																						–	–	–	–	0
W																							–	–	–	0
X																								–	–	0
Y																									–	0
Total	0	2	2	0	2	3	2	2	3	7	9	2	1	2	4	2	3	1	4	1	2	2	4	5	0	64

SYMBOLS

"—" no visits

"w" weak link ($<$ 7 visits/yr)

"s" strong link ($\geq$ 7 visits/yr)

Note: To obtain the total number of
       links for any household: add the total
       at end of the appropriate column and row;
       e.g., the total number of visits made/received
          by household "J" = 7 + 4 = 11.

strong links and 53% of the weak links between the migrant households. Thus, it is a better predictor of strong social relations than of weak social ties.

Two central features of these social ties merit attention. First, long-term residents seldom visit recent arrivals (except kinsmen). As one migrant who had lived in Mexico City since the mid-1940s remarked, "I don't know very many of the young Tzintzuntzeños in the city; when I lived in Tzintzuntzan, most were still children, and some were not yet born." Second, the social relations of long-term migrants are partitioned by socioeconomic status. Those who have achieved significant upward mobility and consider themselves to be professionals rather than workers rarely visit with less affluent migrants. As another migrant declared, "I used to visit with some of the poor migrants, but we have nothing in common anymore. They only want to drink and pass the time; there was nothing for me in the relationship, and I always felt uncomfortable."

The principle of status homogeneity also operates in the kinship domain. Among the 25 migrant households, there are only 30 kinship-related pairs. Of these, 18 maintain visiting relations, with eight strong links and ten weak links. However, in only one case do two kinship-related households with dissimilar socioeconomic statuses maintain a strong link—and they are both recent arrivals. Thus, as Toomey (1970:269) states, "for kin to be contacted frequently and to constitute an influential reference group, they must meet other criteria than merely ascriptive ties of kinship."

To recapitulate, evidence on socioeconomic status, length of urban residence, and kinship relations indicates that homogeneity rather than heterogeneity is the rule for most active links between Tzintzuntzan migrant households. Why is this the case? I believe that the answer has both an economic and a psychological referent.

First, migrants recognize that in order to better their status in the city, they must eventually establish contacts beyond the migrant group. Rather than squander their clientage upon other Tzintzuntzeños, they seek patrons on the job, in the unions, in the government, and in other sectors where opportunity may arise. In the long run, Tzintzuntzeños limit their demands upon their fellow migrants to persons in positions similar to their own. In this sense, the Tzintzuntzan migrants behave much like the residents of working-class neighborhoods studied by Roberts (1970:378) in Guatemala City: "In their personal dealings, most heads of family emphasize that it is desirable to maintain reciprocity in social relations. Most stated that they preferred to borrow money either from those to whom they also lent or under some system of interest payment where the debt relation is a commercial one. Some neighbors commented that they were no longer able to visit certain relatives, since these relatives were rich and they could not hope to return any favors received."

Status homogeneity also has a psychological aspect. Successful migrants, and those who are defined by others as successful even though they may be fairly poor in absolute terms, feel that *envidia* ("envy") is a major reason for the discontinuity of social relations between working-class and professional-level migrants in the capital. One middle-class informant divided the migrant population into two sectors— "*los inferiores*" and "*los superiores*"—on the basis of whether a person earned a living by using his hands or his head. Another felt that the reason no migrant mutual-aid society existed was because "*los maleducados*" ("uneducated," with a sense of "uncultured") fail to appreciate how such an organization would improve their circumstances. This informant neglects to mention the price that they would have to pay in patron-client relations!

The psychological aspects of status homogeneity even influence relations among kinsmen. Thus, one informant explained that he and his brother both live in Mexico City but never visit each other. He claims that his brother is envious of his success in Mexico City. Since the necessary basis of reciprocity is missing, the two brothers avoid one another. This psychological tension also persists between migrants and villagers. For example:

> Gabino Peña is reluctant to have friends who live in Tzintzuntzan visit his apartment in Mexico City. He would prefer to visit them in the village, as he did during Holy Week. His reason is that Tzintzuntzeños criticize his lifestyle—or might do so. He fears that his compadres, for instance, will think he lives well and then ask him for economic assistance.

This case illustrates how friendship tends to be defined in instrumental rather than emotional terms by the Tzintzuntzeños in Mexico City. As Wolf (1966:12), has pointed out, "instrumental friendship may not have been entered into for the purpose of attaining access to resources—natural and social—but the striving for such access becomes vital in it. . . .In contrast to emotional friendship, which is associated with closure of the social circle, instrumental friendship reaches beyond the boundaries of existing sets, and seeks to establish beach-heads in new sets."

Thus, Tzintzuntzan migrants in Mexico City retain only a few specific social relations with their fellows. This does not mean that they fail to adapt to the demands of urban life; on the contrary, they turn to other urbanites in their struggle up the ladder of urban social and economic statuses. Since gathering detailed data on the social relationships of migrants to non-Tzintzuntzeños in the city proved impossible, I shall attempt to convey my impressions of the interaction of the migrants with the urban social system by means of a single, important example—the compadrazgo.

This approach seems valid because migrants themselves feel that the compadrazgo is the primary means by which they formalize "best friend" relationships with non-migrants. In fact, they feel similarly about ties within the migrant group, since geographical separation obviates many traditional advantages of kinship and friendship ties.

THE COMPADRAZGO

The compadrazgo is a system of ritualized personal relations established between the *ahijado*, the *padrinos*, and between the *compadres*. The compadrazgo is usually associated with life cycle rites within the Catholic church, especially those of baptism, confirmation, first communion, and marriage, although compadrazgo ties are also established at other occasions, such as school graduation. Ideally, compadrazgo ties are highly formal, consecrated by use of the term *compadre* or *comadre* (for females) as the mandatory form of address (regardless of pre-existing kinship or friendship ties), and the use of the formal *Usted* rather than the informal *tu*. In actual behavior, compadres may vary widely from the ideal model. Different degrees of informality may exist between sets of compadres according to the degree of daily social contact, kinship ties, socioeconomic status, and other variables.

Types of Compadrazgo

The Village

Foster observes that there are five traditional occasions on which compadrazgo ties are formed: "the baptism of a child, its confirmation, its first communion, its marriage, and the rite known as *de la corona*. Although the first four are associated with the sacraments, and the fifth is validated by a minor religious act, only the first are *de grado*, i.e., of the first importance" (1967:76).

In addition to these fundamentally "sacred" types of compadrazgo, some Tzintzuntzeños also participate in more mundane forms of ritualized social relationships. Since about 1960, when a new school Director came to the community, children have selected adults to serve as padrinos for sixth-grade graduation. This is a short-term tie which compels the sponsor to provide a gift and, in more affluent families, a festive meal in honor of the child. More recently, a few young women have taken up the custom of celebrating their fifteenth birthday with a fiesta. The girls' parents are responsible for the fiesta, but a *madrina* is selected and is expected to provide a nice gift. It appears that the first *quince años* fiesta was held in 1969 in honor of a girl born to migrants living in Mexico City. Since then, at least eight others, in nearly all cases from the most affluent families in the village, have had fifteenth birthday parties and chosen madrinas for the occasion.

Two other ephemeral types of the compadrazgo also occur in Tzintzuntzan: first, some persons select compadres for

FIG. 7-3—The baptismal ceremony strengthens social and economic ties among migrant families through the *compadrazgo*.

blessings of various kinds (e.g., houses, cars, animals); second, at the time of weddings or similar celebrations, some villagers take compadres *de chingere*. This is an emotional, personal tie based on the temporary state of high spirits present at such events and is usually treated as an ongoing "tu-tu" relationship rather than a serious formalized "Usted-Usted" exchange. Both in the case of blessings and de chingere ties, the persons involved may transform their quasi-bond into a stronger compadrazgo tie by selecting one another on more important occasions (e.g., baptisms).

Finally, the last decade has seen an elaboration of the wedding compadrazgo to include several minor ties. The major sponsors are, as always, the padrinos *de velación*; lesser sponsors serve as madrinas *de lazo, de arras, de ramo*, and *de anillos* (i.e., for the cord placed over the bride and groom to signify their sacred union; for the token coins given by the bride to the groom so that the couple will never be poor; for the spray of flowers carried by the bride; and for the rings exchanged by the couple).

It should be clear, nevertheless, that in spite of these recent elaborations upon the local compadrazgo system in Tzintzuntzan, the village has a less developed system of ritual kinship than in many other Mexican communities. For example, Nutini (1976) reports 31 different types of compadrazgo for communities in rural Tlaxcala.

The Migrants

The Tzintzuntzeños in Mexico City represent 35 percent of all emigrants from the village; they are by far the largest concentration in any one locale. Within this diverse migrant population, the types of compadrazgo may be more numerous than in the village. Baptism, confirmation, first communion, and marriage are standard among the migrants. Girls' fifteenth birthday parties, school graduations, the Child Jesus, blessing of an image at church, and blessing of a new home also provide occasions for establishing compadrazgo ties. The explanation for this expansion of types seems to lie with the increased contacts of Tzintzuntzan migrants with other sub-cultural traditions. When the migrants move to the capital they do not reside in tight clusters but live spread among more than forty neighborhoods. This geographical dispersion gives them an exposure to other uses for the compadrazgo beyond the basic types they knew in Tzintzuntzan. As they are asked to serve in these ritual roles, so they in turn begin to use these sponsorships for building affective and instrumental ties with migrants and natives alike.

Tzintzuntzan migrants are not just receptors of new compadrazgo forms; they also serve to disseminate them to the village. In recent years, as we pointed out above, it has become fashionable for Tzintzuntzan children to select pa-

FIG. 7-4—Marriages between Tzintzuntzeños and non-Tzintzuntzeños in Mexico City are becoming more common as the number of migrants increases.

drinos for primary school graduation and for girls to cele-
brate their fifteenth birthdays with parties sponsored by a
madrina. While these forms of compadrazgo are not de grado,
they do show the influence of *urban* forces upon an institution once conceived of by anthropologists as preeminently
rural and traditional.

Choices of Compadres

The compadrazgo is the primary means through which Tzintzuntzan migrants in Mexico City formalize and strengthen ties
with migrants as well as other urban residents. Comparison of
the compadrazgo among Tzintzuntzeños in Mexico City with
that among villagers illustrates the ways in which migrants
utilize it to improve personal social networks in the urban
situation. I gathered information on 111 cases of baptismal
godparents and 61 cases of confirmation godparents for migrant children born in Mexico City. [For purposes of comparison, I use Foster's (1969) village sample of 788 cases
which covers approximately the same time period.]
    Tzintzuntzan migrants appear to follow closely the "rules"
for choosing godparents which operate in the village. For
instance, in Tzintzuntzan 78% of baptismal godparents were
married couples, 33% were relatives, and 52% of the relatives
chosen were siblings of the child's parents. The comparable
figures for Tzintzuntzeños in Mexico City are 79% married
couples, 26% relatives, and 52% siblings. Furthermore, only
31% of baptismal godparents in our migrant sample were
chosen among fellow migrants, and just 17% were persons
living in the village at the time of the ceremony, although
when villagers are chosen this nearly always occurs when the
ceremony is also held in Tzintzuntzan rather than in the city.
In contrast, only 13% of the village sample examined by
Foster chose godparents from outside Tzintzuntzan.
    From the villagers' viewpoint, the compadrazgo serves to
intensify social bonds with kinsmen (and persons who are

already compadres); it extends ties to unrelated villagers and to persons outside Tzintzuntzan. In contrast, the migrants use the compadrazgo to intensify relations with the village and with their fellow migrants. This intensification includes kinsmen, compadres, and friends. Extension of social relationships involves establishing ties beyond the migrant group and thus brings the Tzintzuntzeños into the social orbits defined by neighborhoods, jobs, and associations, and other urban socioeconomic categories. The extent to which the migrants use the compadrazgo mechanism to build bridges to non-migrants is shown in Table 7-4.

Relative Status of Compadres

In Tzintzuntzan baptismal godparents usually (75%) have the same socioeconomic status as the child's parents and if unequal are likely to be of higher status than the parents (21%). Among the migrants in Mexico City, only 56% of the baptismal and confirmation godparents are of the same socioeconomic status. Thirty-one percent are of higher status, and 12% are lower. Both of these vertical dimensions of the compadrazgo are thus accentuated in the urban setting. It is likely that as Tzintzuntzan develops a more elaborate class structure, which is currently underway (Kemper and Foster 1975:74), the vertical aspects of the compadrazgo within the community will also become more important. For the present, it is clear that the migrants in Mexico City use the compadrazgo (both in asking others to serve and in accepting other's requests to serve) as a device for establishing patron-client ties. Usually, the Tzintzuntzeños in the capital try to improve their opportunities for upward mobility by asking non-Tzintzuntzan urbanites, whereas most ties among the migrant group are between persons of similar status. In this respect, they behave as do their village counterparts, who emphasize same-status ties within the community and higher-status ties with outsiders.

TABLE 7-4
Compadrazgo Choices among Tzintzuntzan Migrants

Compadrazgo Tie With	Occasion: Baptism	Occasion: Confirmation	Total	%
Village				
a. Relatives	8	4	12	
b. Friends	8	6	14	
Sub-total	16	10	26	16
Fellow Migrants				
a. Relatives	6	4	10	
b. Friends	15	3	18	
Sub-total	21	7	28	17
Other Mexico City Residents				
a. In-laws	9	7	16	
b. Neighbors	28	15	43	
c. Work companions	18	5	23	
d. Miscl./insufficient data	13	11	24	
Sub-total	68	38	106	65
Non-Mexico City In-laws	1	2	3	2
Total	106	57	163	100

Interpersonal Relations among Compadres

In Tzintzuntzan the compadrazgo functions to cement commercial ties as well as to build a cohesive social structure. These commercial ties are manipulated with outsiders as well as with fellow villagers through the compadrazgo system. For example, it is common for middlemen in the pottery industry to set up ties with distributors and retailers in other communities.

Because Tzintzuntzan is still a small-scale community, compadres are in frequent, even daily contact with each other. As a result, the opportunities for mutual assistance and potential conflict are almost always present. This is, of course, less so in the cases where villagers seek outsiders as compadres. The balance between daily contacts, usually with one's peers, and frequent contacts, such as with patrons in other communities or in government agencies, is not always easy to maintain. However, those villagers able to maintain this Janus-like style of compadrazgo appear to be among the most successful of the people in Tzintzuntzan.

Because of the geographical dispersion of the migrants and the wide distances between their homes and jobs, the visiting patterns are rather different from the daily interaction possible in the village. Nevertheless, compadres are much more prone to visit one another than are friends or even relatives, although distances to be travelled influence all types of visiting. In general, we can state that the compadres have much closer relationships than do other Tzintzuntzan migrants with each other. During a period of twelve months prior to being interviewed, only 26% of the compadres surveyed had not been visited by their respective compadres, 48% had been seen occasionally, 9% had been visited frequently, and 17% had received regular visits. It should be noted that in 4% of the cases, recorded as "none," the compadrazgo tie had dissolved because of the death of the godchild, in accord with the common attitude that "*muerto el ahijado, acabó el compadrazgo*" ("when the godchild has died, the godparenthood is finished").

Significantly, no pairs of compadres lived in the same household in the city. Informants explain this phenomenon by noting that serious quarrels between compadres would be disastrous to the sanctity of their relationship, and that to choose compadres from persons living in the same household would invite trouble. This pattern of avoidance is also common in Tzintzuntzan.

If visiting patterns are the social manifestation of the strength of compadrazgo ties, then modes of address provide clues to the institution's symbolic qualities. Although the cultural ideals indicate that compadres use formal types of address (e.g., *Usted* compadre), a substantial minority (38%) continue to use "mixed" or informal modes of address after the compadrazgo ties are established.

The formality of the compadrazgo relationship depends on the distinction between "horizontal" and "vertical" ties, the previous kinship relation, and the degree of *confianza* between the two parties. Among pairs of compadres having unequal status, persons in the inferior position use the formal *Usted* mode of address and refer to the other parties as "compadres" rather than by first names. By contrast, persons in the superior position use the informal *tu* mode of address and the first names of their compadres.

Despite the ideal model that compadrazgo ties should obviate previous kinship ties of mutual trust and confidence, among Tzintzuntzeños in the city, formality is often observed only by inference. Several times I observed compadres who began conversations and visits with the proper, formal modes of address only to shift later into informal, highly personalized discussions after the initial bow toward tradition. Then, when the compadres parted company they returned to the ritualized forms of behavior in order to reestablish the "correct" relationship between themselves. Informality is most often found among siblings or other close kin, but in these cases their spouses (connected only by the tenous in-law ties) follow the formal modes of address. Such "mixed" behavior within the same pairs of compadres validates and strengthens in-law ties at the same time that it has little effect on kinship ties.

SUMMARY

The social organization of the migrants has a flexibility compatible with the diversity of life styles in Mexico City. The combination of kinship, friendship, and compadrazgo relations binds neighbors, work companions, employers and employees, fellow migrants, and villagers into instrumental and affective alliances. These alliances may be both vertical and horizontal, both intensive and extensive. Thus, the migrants enjoy a range of social options, from the most reserved formal posture of *respeto* to the most informal personal stance of *confianza*. Moreover, because many types of social relationships involve no (or few) permanent obligations, most of a person's ties remain latent. Only a few of one's potential contacts during the life cycle receive special attention; the rest are recognized as of less (or temporary) importance within an individual's social and economic spheres.

This is particularly important in the urban setting where geographical and class separation tend to isolate migrant family groups from each other and frequent residential mobility also limits their interaction with non-migrant neighbors.

Notes for Chapter 7

1. The statutes of the "Agrupación de Tzintzuntzeños radicados fuera de su Pueblo" (Association of Tzintzuntzeños living outside of the Village) emphasize contact with the home community, dedication to spiritual values, and integration of the migrant group beyond Tzintzuntzan. The statutes read as follows (my translation): (I.) The "Association . . ." accepts and supports as its Patron the "Señor del Rescate" of Tzintzuntzan, Michoacán, because he embodies its desires and spirit; (II.) As evidence of this devotion to the "Señor del Rescate," the Association will support and conduct a most solemn pilgrimage to his sanctuary in February each year; (III.) It is the duty of each Association member to present an offering during the yearly pilgrimage, either in person or through a relative living in the village; (IV.) We repeat our faith in the "Señor del Rescate," accepting the sacrifices of our forefathers for the blessing of our children; (V.) We consider it appropriate that our children attend our gatherings so that they can observe and follow the example of their parents; (VI.) We reject absolutely the presence of intoxicating beverages in all of our acts; (VII.) We want the presence of the "Señor del Rescate" in our homes to be the basis for the spiritual formation of our families and to serve as a means of bringing all the members into harmony; to that end we propose the

practice of the Rosary, Masses, Communion, or that we develop our own private prayers that we teach our children; (VIII.) We will struggle to maintain a closeness that will permit us to help one another in our physical, spiritual, social, and cultural problems. (IX.) The "Association . . ." promises to give its monthly donation for the public welfare in accord with the members' personal economic resources; (X.) We accept the responsibility to carry out the Association's resolutions, always taking into account our particular circumstances but always putting forth our best efforts.

CHAPTER 8

CONCLUSION

The aspect of urbanism which has been of primary interest to the anthropologist is migration and migrant adjustment. He first became concerned with urbanization through following the peasant to the city.   Goode (1970:152)

During the twenty-five years since Lewis's pioneering field-work in Mexico City, in which he suggested that migrants from Tepoztlán undergo "urbanization without breakdown" (1952), anthropologists and other social scientists have devoted considerable attention to cityward migration in Latin America. The causes and patterns of migration, its effects on communities of origin and destination, the characteristics of the migrants, and a wide range of urban adaptations have been investigated. Nevertheless, we are still without a satisfactory theoretical model which will predict individual adaptations within the migration process. Several recent commentators have been concerned with the theoretical underpinnings of research on migration and adaptation (Singer 1973; Oliveira and Stern 1974; Sauers 1974; Du Toit 1975; Cardona and Simmons 1975; Buechler 1975; Midgett 1976; Weaver and Downing 1976; Arizpe 1976). Their concerns are summarized by Shaw (1975:136) who, after a lengthy review and bibliography of the current migration literature, cautions that the slow process of relating the "who" and "why" of migration to its underlying structural and behavioral determinants has just begun.

RESEARCH DESIGNS

A number of different research designs have been used by anthropologists and other social scientists to describe and analyze cityward migration and adaptation. A brief assessment of the most common research designs will show their particular strengths and weaknesses, especially insofar as the type of study conducted influences the quantity and variety of data available to the investigator. The following discussion also will indicate that, although the approach used in my research among the Tzintzuntzan migrants in Mexico City is only one of several possible research designs, it has several advantages for understanding migration and adaptation as processual strategies.

National Studies

Studying cityward migration at the national (or international) level requires that data be available on *all* migrants—regardless of place of origin—to *all* cities of destination. This approach understandably involves extensive use of census data rather than direct field observations (Weaver and Downing 1976). A major problem with this approach is that examination of cityward migration is often subsumed by regional, state, and municipal levels of analysis. Moreover, the problem of defining the "rural" and "urban" sectors of the society is burdensome (C.E.E.D. 1970). In this research design the orientation is toward migration as mass behavior; information on individual adaptation in new environments is usually absent and, even when provided, is so aggregated that it is of little use. National studies can provide good longitudinal data on migration trends, but the trends are actually no more than points on a graph. They reveal decision-making in the migration process only in the aggregate.

City-Based Studies

The migration of *all* persons who go to a *single* city (or, less often, to a set of cities) can be examined by using census data, by conducting extensive sample surveys, or by combining these two research strategies. While the investigator's concern remains with the overall migration process, considerable data about individual careers may be obtained. This category of studies, like national-level research, often emphasizes comparisons of migrants and urban natives to ascertain how well the migrants, whatever their origins, compete in the urban arena (Balán, Browning, and Jelín 1973; Herrick 1965). The focus on the urban context of adaptation limits the researcher's awareness of variability among communities of origin. The use of life histories, however, in combination with other sample survey techniques, partially counteracts this weakness.

A related type of city-based investigation involves fieldwork in a restricted setting, such as a squatter settlement, working-class neighborhood, or central city slum zone. This concentration on a subunit of the city permits a finer-grained picture of migration and adaptation but at the expense of overall representativeness. As a result, the best studies of the "neighborhood" *genre* attempt to link the particular location investigated into the broader urban system (Chance 1971; Germani 1961; Lomnitz 1975; Patch 1961; Peattie 1968; Whiteford 1976). Intermediate to the single-neighborhood study and the large-scale sample surveys are the multi-neighborhood investigations which combine intensive ethnographic fieldwork with sample survey techniques (Cornelius 1975; Jackson 1973; Roberts 1970). City-based studies may provide excellent longitudinal data on migration and adaptation. Unfortunately, however, too many remain one-shot, static descriptions of specific urban environments.

Village-Based Studies

A few social scientists have studied migration in a *single* community (or region) of origin and concentrated on the impact of *all* out-migration upon that community. This approach is especially popular among anthropologists, who find it to be a logical extension of their interest in the modernization of peasant villages. Emphasizing direct observation rather than the use of sample survey or census data, such projects (Brandes 1975; Butterworth 1969; Gonzalez 1969) yield valuable information on the way in which non-migrants adapt to changing conditions resulting from the departure of other members of the population. Thus, village-based studies are useful complements to the city-based and national-level studies of migration and adaptation, although they may be unrepresentative of the larger class of rural communities of origin. The depth of ethnographic knowledge obtained in this type of study may compensate for this deficiency. This is especially true when a fieldworker makes a commitment to conduct a long-term study of emigration and its effects on the community.

Village-City Studies

The final approach to studying migration and adaptation is that used in my fieldwork among Tzintzuntzan migrants—examination of migrants from a *single* community of origin to a *single* urban destination. This research design represents the antithesis of the national-level study in which all migrants to all cities are investigated. Projects of the village-city category are usually done in two stages: first, the fieldworker does a comprehensive community study; second, he follows the migrants to a city where he can assess their adaptation to urban life. Rarely, an investigator will begin work in the city and then move to a village, if he can find one which sends a large stream of migrants to that particular city (Browning and Feindt 1969). In either approach, the emphasis is on the individual as a significant actor in a system that includes both the communities of origin and destination. Given an adequate ethnographic record for the community of origin, it is possible to generate a detailed longitudinal study of migration and adaptation. For example, Lewis's work among the

Tepoztlán migrants in Mexico City persisted throughout the 1950s and 1960s. In my own case, I anticipate working with Tzintzuntzan migrants (and villagers) over an entire generation, measuring the impact of migration on their home community, on Mexico City as an urban destination, and on them as members of Mexican society.

It should be apparent that the several research designs discussed here offer diverse, but complementary, perspectives on the processes of migration and adaptation. Moreover, researchers can shift from one research design to another as their interests change or expand. Thus, Lewis began with a village-city study, shifted to a city-based study of all migrants in a particular slum zone, and finally took up the problem of urban poverty without regard to whether individuals were migrants or urban natives. Indeed, a sorely neglected area of study involves the second generation; that is, what happens to the migrants' children who are born and reared in the urban setting? This is a question which we will take up later in this chapter.

I believe that although none of the research designs considered here deals rigorously with *all* dimensions of cityward migration and adaptation, the village-city approach offers advantages for in-depth longitudinal analysis which compensate for its potential unrepresentativeness. As Shaw (1975:138) has stated, the data needed for a comprehensive analysis of individual decision-making "include longitudinal studies encompassing socioeconomic characteristics of migrants, migration histories, and small group research." Indeed, the considerable variations in individual strategies of migration and adaptation are revealed more eloquently in this type of field-based study than in those which depend heavily on macro-level quantitative data.

MIGRATION: PROCESS AND STRATEGY

Most early discussions of migrant adaptation in Latin American cities were couched in terms of the Great

Dichotomy, variously designated "folk-urban," "remote-modern," "traditional-modern," or "rural-urban." Regardless of its label, this model assumes that differences in population size and environmental setting between "rural" and "urban" groups result in important social, economic, cultural, and psychological dissimilarities. As Bonilla (1964:187) has observed, this view may lead to a "facile dualism that makes the city representative of everything modern and progressive and attributes the total burden of backwardness to rural areas." A corollary suggests that cityward migrants from "rural" areas ought to experience major difficulties in adjusting to "urban" culture. Such difficulties are supposed to result in culture conflicts, disorganization of traditional lifestyles, personal anomie and alienation, and breakdown of primary group affiliations.

In contrast, I believe that the modernization of contemporary Mexico is creating a single system in which villages and cities each play important roles. The dominance of metropolitan areas, especially Mexico City, cannot be denied, but it is necessary to keep a balanced perspective. As Midgett (1976:268) points out, "despite the intrinsic interest of a microscopic examination of a Mexican villager's adaptation to Mexico City, the recognition that he was and is a part of a larger economic, political, and social system is crucial to an appraisal of the adaptive process as it applies to him and his fellows." Similar arguments have been made by Guillet and Uzzell (1976), Sauers (1974), McGee (1975), Hanson and Simmons (1968), and Graves (1966).

This perspective is especially appropriate in the case of Tzintzuntzan and its migrants in Mexico City. As the "urbanization" of the Mexican countryside has continued into the 1970s, many villagers have expanded their worldviews and reconsidered their options. As a result, migration has become a routine matter for the people of Tzintzuntzan. Between 1930 and 1940, when 10.6% of all Mexicans were moving across state boundaries, only a handful of Tzintzuntzeños ventured outside of Michoacán. In contrast, about 15% of all village households had one or more members leave the state between 1960 and 1970. This proportion is in line with the current national average of 14.5%, although it may be slightly lower than the average for other communities in Michoacán. For this period, the state had the nation's highest net emigration, with a negative imbalance of 260,928 persons (Weaver and Downing 1976:43, 47).

Although large-scale migration is recent in Tzintzuntzan, its migratory patterns already are becoming stabilized. Thus, what Balán, Browning, and Jelín (1973:169) found for the northern Mexican community of Cedral now applies to Tzintzuntzan: "Residential mobility is fundamental to an understanding of the life and institutions of this community .... The result is that migration rightfully should be seen as continuous activity, nearly always simultaneously involving many people in communities both of origin and destination."

It is also important to recognize that migration is not always directly related to local, regional, or national economic conditions. Tzintzuntzeños select destinations based on both their perception of available jobs and their knowledge that friends and relatives will help them settle in the city. The comparative literature stresses the powerful role of kinship and social ties in the migration process (Balán, Browning, and Jelín 1973:159-164; Cornelius 1975:22; Buechler 1975:287; Graves and Graves 1974:128-132; Whiteford 1976:23). In this regard, we properly may speak of migration strategies through which villagers manipulate available contacts to improve their current situations.

During the past two decades, the people of Tzintzuntzan have learned to treat migration as an option to remaining in the village. In the process, the community's standards of appropriate behavior have been changing. The demise of the closed, defensive posture characterized by the "image of limited good" (Foster 1965, 1972) can be traced directly to the impact of external forces, including Tzintzuntzan migrants.

Moreover, "return migration doubtless serves an important, if sometimes overlooked, function as a kind of sorting device that removes . . . some of those who are unsuccessful or dissatisfied or both" (Balán, Browning, and Jelín 1973:170). As we have seen, returning to the village need not imply failure; it can simply show that, for the present, an individual or family prefers conditions in the village to those in the metropolis. The impact of these returned migrants on Tzintzuntzan has yet to be examined in detail, but this topic certainly merits further study.

Increasing access to the outside world, fostered in part through a variety of migration strategies, has transformed Tzintzuntzan during a single generation. In a recent study of the impact of migration on a Spanish village, Brandes (1975:183) reached a similar conclusion: "All of these changes signify a cultural revolution in the countryside, a revolution that has all but totally eliminated the distinctive, localized beliefs and customs found in peasant villages of the past." That is the price of modernization willingly paid by Tzintzuntzan and thousands of other Mexican villages.

MIGRANT SELECTIVITY

The evaluation of migration and adaptation is a function of the observer's vantage point. When migrants are studied in the urban context they often appear to be "of lower status, less competent, ill-prepared for dealing with urban complexities and ambiguities" (Fried 1969:46). On the other hand, when compared to non-migrants in their home communities, they seem to be those best qualified for success. Migrant selectivity, therefore, is relative. Moreover, the evidence is persuasive that selectivity declines over time. This point is well-documented in the Monterrey Mobility Study:

"This dynamic feature of selectivity is perhaps the most significant . . . of our findings, and it was interpreted in the context of 'pioneer' versus 'mass' migration. An important reason for the decline in positive selectivity is to be found in the idea of a static and diminishing reservoir of potential migrants" (Balán, Browning, and Jelín 1973:168).

The case of Tzintzuntzan suggests, however, that migrant selectivity may decline even when the pool of potential migrants is not "static and diminishing." The village population continues to increase, and the current generation receives an education superior to that available to the "pioneer" migrants of the 1940s and 1950s. Unfortunately, educational superiority to yesterday's migrants is not what matters. Today's migrants must compete in cities whose capacity for absorbing additional population is being strained. Thus, an important advantage of being a "pioneer" migrant seems to lie in having achieved job security during a period of unparalleled economic prosperity in Mexican society.

Changing patterns of selectivity also affect the ways in which Tzintzuntzeños use their social networks in the migration process. In this regard, Graves and Graves (1974:128) offer a useful distinction between individualistic and group-oriented strategies: "We can consider as *individualistic* those strategies where a migrant relies essentially on his own resources or his own initiative for a solution. If he uses institutional resources made available by the host community, he does so as an individual or nuclear household head. By contrast, in *group-oriented* strategies the migrant turns for help to other people, usually kinsmen, fellow villagers, or migrants from his own ethnic group."

As Tinztzuntzan has shifted from "pioneer" to "mass" migration during the past two decades, villagers have learned to use the migrants who preceded them to find urban housing and jobs. The early adventurers were not able to use a group-oriented strategy; they were usually alone in the metropolis and had to rely on their own skills. Their ultimate success made it possible for many more villagers to enter the urban scene. There may soon be, however, a conflict between the migrants' willingness to help their fellow villagers and their interest in helping their own children succeed in the city. If the system can no longer absorb an increasing number of new arrivals, the issue of migrant selectivity may become even more critical. Indeed, social scientists eventually may conclude that the migration processes and strategies common during the 1960s and 1970s were not universal but merely adaptations to a specific combination of social, economic, and political conditions.

ADAPTATION: PROCESS AND STRATEGY

For the migrant, adaptation to city life is not a unitary process. Tzintzuntzeños may migrate to Mexico City, but they occupy narrowly circumscribed "niches" related to home, job, school, neighborhood, etc. Each migrant, therefore, perceives the city idiosyncratically and follows a particular role path (Hanson and Simmons 1968) in his urban experiences. In this section I will summarize my findings on the principal residential, organizational, and occupational strategies employed by the Tzintzuntzan migrants. Although these strategies are treated separately, they represent a constellation of evolving, overlapping options available to migrants and natives alike. The sum of these strategies represents the adaptation process for specific individuals and, when treated in the aggregate, the entire Tzintzuntzan migrant population in the capital.

Residential Strategies

The migrants' first residence in Mexico City is usually arranged through friends and relatives. The availability of housing is also influenced by governmental and private sectors. For instance, the prohibition on new residential subdivisions within the Federal District, in effect from 1952 to 1970 (Cornelius 1975:27), restricted the housing options for new arrivals. Rent control policies in the central city have had similar effects. As a result, most Tzintzuntzeños now live near the metropolitan periphery.

Limitations on the urban housing stock have encouraged many migrants to reconsider traditional family and household arrangements. Although the conjugal family remains important, enclaves of extended families have sprouted in several *colonias*. Renting adjacent apartments in a *vecindad* is structurally the same as buying an empty lot with kinsmen and sharing the burden of construction. These strategies are not simple recreations of village residential patterns; they reflect the migrants' efforts to conserve fiscal and social resources in a crowded metropolitan environment.

Organizational Strategies

The basic organizational strategy among the Tzintzuntzan migrants is the individualistic dyadic contract. Formal groups have been unimportant for the migrants as a "community," although the recent creation of a voluntary association offers an avenue for group action. Tzintzuntzeños in Mexico City emphasize ties of friendship, kinship, and *compadrazgo* rather than membership in neighborhood associations, political parties, or unions.

The newly established *Agrupación* of Tzintzuntzan migrants did not exist in 1969-1970 or 1974, during the first two periods of my fieldwork, and it may not survive if it fails to unite the migrants. Can this association, founded by a socially-minded school principal nearing retirement age, bridge the present social barriers between working-class and middle-class migrants? Can it strengthen the migrants' ties to the village? Can it give the migrants' children a sense of group identity? Only long-term research will answer these questions.

The Tzintzuntzeños in the capital have never united to press for political favors, economic benefits, or social services. Their geographical and social diversity prevents them from organizing as squatter settlement populations frequently do. Nevertheless, several migrants have helped the villagers manipulate state and federal political systems so that a secondary school could be constructed in Tzintzuntzan. Perhaps their success in this affair will lead to other village-oriented activities, probably through the Agrupación.

Emphasis on the migrants' individualistic social behavior does not mean that they are lost in an impersonal urban world. On the contrary, many belong to unions, participate in neighborhood organizations, or serve in parish church groups. This occurs on an individual or familial basis; it does not bring the migrants together as a community. Migrant families occasionally gather for weddings, baptisms, funerals, fiestas, and important civil or religious holidays.

Social interaction of the Tzintzuntzeños in Mexico City involve ties with fellow migrants and other urban residents. The strategy of social interaction among the migrants stresses status homogeneity; that between migrants and non-migrants emphasizes status heterogeneity. In the process of upward mobility and socioeconomic adaptation, some migrants have cut themselves off from the rest of the migrant group, including their kinsmen. They no longer care what migrants and villagers say about their egoistic behavior. Their social and psychological support derives from familial, neighborhood, and occupational groups. Thus, migrant social relations may be quite complex, involving changing combinations of individualistic and group-oriented strategies.

Occupational Strategies

The success of the Tzintzuntzan migrants' occupational strategies is reflected in their extremely low unemployment rate. Assistance provided by friends and relatives usually gives way to more powerful connections formed at work or in the union. Major tensions faced by migrants involve job security and salary. They try to minimize job changes, so that they can obtain tenure and its benefits as soon as possible.

Migration from village to metropolis usually results in occupational shifts which give the appearance of upward mobility (CEPAL 1975:230). As Shannon and Shannon (1968:55) have observed, "the migrant may be working at the lowest level in the urban industrial society but at a higher level on the scale of occupations for the total society only because the urban industrial society has relatively few positions comparable to those in the rural or small town society from which he came." A number of Tzintzuntzan migrants working in the capital as domestic servants, construction workers, or small shopkeepers operate in economic niches similar to those in the village; others experience a series of occupational changes.

Certain attitudes accompany the occupational strategies of low-income and middle-class migrants. The former stress the differential *availability of work* in the city; the latter emphasize the relative *opportunity to progress*. The following comments illustrate these different attitudes toward urban economic life.

Low-income respondent:

"Life is hard here in the city, particularly for a poor person unfamiliar with city ways. But, we don't leave here because we can survive better than back in Tzintzuntzan."

Middle-class respondent:

"In the city a path is open for one's career, to get what is necessary to lead a good life, and to obtain luxuries. And, above all, here one can progress."

PSYCHOLOGICAL DIMENSIONS OF ADAPTATION

According to Brody (1969:14), "adaptation in the psychological sense refers to the process of establishing and maintaining a relatively stable reciprocal relationship with the environment." Moving to Mexico City not only involves new residential, organizational, and occupational strategies, it also may require modification of an individual's worldview. If a migrant holds values inappropriate for city life, "it is just as likely that these are not *rural* attitudes, but attitudes acquired in the process of interacting in a situation where he has been defined as an inferior" (Shannon and Shannon 1968:63; emphasis added). On the basis of extensive research in Mexico and Brazil, Kahl (1968:18-19) concluded: "Marginal men at the very bottom of the status hierarchy, even in big cities, often behave like peasants, for they too are subject to manipulation beyond their control . . . . Low status makes a man traditional . . . even more than does provincial location."

Tzintzuntzeños near the bottom of the socioeconomic scale in Mexico City face pressures and frustrations which parallel those of the poorest peasants. For these few, their concern is day-to-day survival, not upward mobility (Lomnitz 1975; Whiteford 1976). In contrast, most Tzintzuntzan migrants have steady jobs that provide a minimal income for immediate needs and long-term prospects. Accordingly, they have a more optimistic worldview in which the balance between present and future is pragmatically understood. Finally, a small but growing number of Tzintzuntzeños in the capital have achieved middle-class, professional status. Unfortunately, their "social climbing" is often accompanied by tensions and frustrations. If it seems odd that the poorest and most affluent Tzintzuntzan migrants experience more psychological malaise than those in an intermediate working-class position, we should recall that perceived status may be as significant as objective status.

These observations are reflected in responses to several TAT pictures, especially the "blank card" and the "rope-climber."

CARD 16—Blank card.

NARRATOR—A 29-year-old, economically marginal migrant

Once I lived with a friend who was always happy, always smiling. We got through our poverty and hard times happily. He became rich and now I think, "Why won't I get wealthy if he could?" And I ponder it. He had a similar beginning, but luck came his way. I tell myself that I shouldn't complain about his good fortune, but for me to get rich—well, it will never happen.

CARD 17BM—A naked man is climbing a rope.

NARRATOR—A 25-year-old, tenured factory worker

Here is a figure grabbing onto a rope. Earlier he was in a dungeon or in jail. To escape from the jail he took off his clothes to make a rope. But, he didn't worry about going naked in the street; what made him happy was the pure air he breathed, the sun he saw again, and the people around him.

NARRATOR—A 24-year-old, rising professional

This young man's dream was to become a great athlete and to represent his country. From youth he began training in sports, and eventually chose gymnastics as his specialty. He dedicated his life to this endeavor, and dreamed of being in the Olympics. Such was his dedication that he managed to achieve this goal, but the following occurred: when in training he fell from a height, and his dreams were finished. The misfortune ended the chance to represent his country, since the results were not just psychological but physical as well. So, he became useless for the rest of his life.

Why does such psychological adaptation vary among poor, working-class, and middle-class migrants? The frustration of economically marginal migrants accurately reflects their limited chances for upward mobility. In contrast, those with tenured jobs in industry or government have reason to be optimistic; some even hope to see their children become middle-class professionals. Finally, those migrants who have achieved middle-class standing are victims of the "revolution of growing expectations" in contemporary Mexico (Cardona and Simmons 1975:34). They are close enough to the elite to appreciate the meaning of wealth and power; they are also close enough to their village origins to remember the problems of poverty.

The dilemma of middle-class migrants is especially important for understanding problems of urban adaptation. They often find themselves caught in the middle, with lofty aspirations and limited economic resources. The older middle-class migrants tend to be satisfied with their present positions, and are less concerned with improving their economic situation than are their younger counterparts. While both groups wish to establish a base for their childrens' professional careers, the younger middle-class migrants need not worry about this for a decade or two.

Most Tzintzuntzan migrants have a strong future orientation. Only those in economically marginal positions feel insecure about their prospects, and even these migrants hope that their current sacrifices will result in a better life for their children. Like their village counterparts, the migrants have great faith in the power of education to raise their offspring another step up the ladder of success. If a primary school credential was enough to lift them out of the village fields and into a factory, they reason, then a secondary or college degree should certainly bring their children a professional position. Unfortunately, the gap between working class and middle class is too wide for many people to bridge in a single generation. Moreover, it is likely that the competition for civil service jobs and professional positions (e.g., doctors, law-yers, engineers) in the capital will become increasingly stren-uous in the next two decades.

It may be that, in order to fulfill their dreams of upward mobility, young migrants will have to leave Mexico City to take posts in provincial cities and towns. If this occurs, then the migrants' optimism about the future will be rewarded, although not as they anticipated. More importantly, the pool of professional talent in Mexico City will be distributed among other communities in need of their services. This heavy flow of migrants to the capital would represent only one stage in their movement in Mexico's urban system. Can higher education help to diffuse Tzintzuntzeños throughout the nation? If so, then what psychological adaptations would occur among these individuals reared in Tzintzuntzan, edu-cated in Mexico City, and subsequently shifted to, say Vera-cruz? Only by following these migrants beyond the capital can we discover the answers.

THE FUTURE

In this volume I have stressed three complementary dimen-sions of migration and adaptation: changes in the community of origin (Chapters 1 and 2); changes in the community of destination (Chapters 3 and 4); and changes in the migrant population (Chapters 5, 6, and 7). The ethnographic data collected among the migrants since 1969, Foster's data on Tzintzuntzan since 1945, and governmental census data since 1930 provide a reasonably complete picture of the progress of the current generation of Tzintzuntzeños in the village and in the metropolis. What lies ahead for the next generation?

Pessimists would respond that the Mexican economic "miracle" of the past twenty-five years is finished and with it any hope of continued prosperity. They would point to the recent problems of inflation and devaluation as supporting evidence. They would also argue that Mexico City, with its burgeoning population, air pollution, and water shortages, can tolerate no more in-migration. They might even suggest that the Tzintzuntzan migrants in the capital gain economic progress (illusory at best because of the city's high living costs) at the expense of their affinity with their home community. They might conclude that the recent outpouring of Tzintzuntzeños into Mexico City is just a temporary solution to the nation's structural inequalities and, therefore, does no more to solve the nation's problems than did the bracero program.

In contrast, optimists would respond that Mexico has great opportunities to improve the national quality of life in the next two decades. They would cite the recent petroleum and natural gas discoveries as examples. They would argue that Mexico City's problems, with its current 12 million or its projected 32 million people, are not insurmountable. They might even suggest that increased in-migration of well prepared citizens, such as the positively selected Tzintzuntzeños, helps to improve the urban economy while relieving the countryside of labor force competition. They might conclude that the continuing emigration of Tzintzuntzeños into Mexico City, linked to a redistribution of these migrants to other cities, will provide sufficient remittances to keep their home community solvent.

I am neither pessimist nor optimist. As a social scientist, I still know too little to predict the path of nations, much less that of individuals. I do think, however, that the next generation will provide answers to a number of intriguing questions.

In Tzintzuntzan, the community of origin: Will the population growth rate level off, or even decline, so that emigration becomes less significant? Will better local educational opportunities keep more adolescents at home or just encourage them to pursue collegiate careers elsewhere? Will emigration have a long-term positive or negative effect on the villagers' perceptions of the local opportunity structure? Will Tzintzuntzan be able to reabsorb a large quantity of migrants who return as retirees, or because they lost their jobs in the city?

In Mexico City, the community of destination: Can the metropolis be contained? Can the environmental and housing problems be solved? Can the city continue to offer a "better" life to migrants and natives?

Among the Tzintzuntzan migrants: Will they continue to move to the capital in preference to other destinations? Will they retain a sense of affiliation with the village? Will they continue to prosper economically? Will their nascent voluntary association flourish? Will the migrants attain their goal of owning homes, educating their children, and prospering?

Tzintzuntzan migrants are not passive pawns moved by impersonal economic and political forces. They are active agents in shaping their own destinies and, in turn, that of contemporary Mexico. The wide range of strategies they employ in the migration and adaptation processes demonstrates their commitment to be the last generation of the past and the first generation of the future.

APPENDIX
FIELDWORK: A PERSONAL PERSPECTIVE

In 1967, while writing up the results of summer research on the peasant marketplace in Pátzcuaro, Michoacán, I became interested in the participation of local communities in Mexican urbanization. Subsequent discussions with George Foster, then my graduate adviser at the University of California (Berkeley), led me to undertake fieldwork for the doctoral dissertation among Tzintzuntzan migrants in Mexico City. I have now spent on that project about twenty months of field research from 1969 through 1976. Plans for future research include year-long revisits on a decennial schedule in addition to a number of shorter trips.

In this appendix, I shall examine the development of the project so far, discuss the plans for further fieldwork, and consider the study's theoretical and methodological implications for other anthropologists and social scientists interested in comparative urbanization research and theory.

HISTORY OF THE RESEARCH

From the outset, my research has been a continuation of Foster's long-term fieldwork in Tzintzuntzan. Our decision that I should carry out this fieldwork for a dissertation was due primarily to the availability of substantial data on the migrants' home community. Thus, I would be able to concentrate on a single phase of what for other ethnographers is usually a time-consuming, two-stage project. Just as Oscar Lewis had followed migrants from Tepoztlán to Mexico City, so I would go from Tzintzuntzan to the capital. Indeed, my decision to do the project was influenced by Lewis's (1952:41) long-ignored suggestion that follow-up studies of migrants from villages like Tzintzuntzan (i.e., communities already subjected to intensive ethnographic fieldwork) would yield valuable comparative data on Mexican urbanization.

FIELDWORK IN 1969 AND 1970

Mexico City was selected as the field site because Tzintzuntzan emigrants share with many Mexican peasants, including those of Tepoztlán, a preference for settling in the capital. Thus, not only would I find enough migrants to make the study worthwhile, I would be able to compare my findings directly with those of Lewis and other scholars while avoiding the arduous task of locating Tzintzuntzeños in a number of Mexican cities. Under these conditions, I conducted fieldwork in Mexico City, with several brief trips to the village, from April 1969 to August 1970.

Since the methods, techniques, and preliminary results of the 1969-1970 research have been reported in detail elsewhere (Kemper 1974), I will discuss here only a few issues as they relate to my long-term fieldwork among the Tzintzuntzan migrants.

Selecting a Place to Live

All anthropologists face the problem of finding accommodations compatible with their field situation. In my case, after two weeks of living in hotels and rooming houses, we rented a furnished apartment near the center of the city. Having an apartment independent of all of the migrants had immediate advantages, and disadvantages, for the 1969-1970 fieldwork: on the one hand, it gave us a place away from the constant demands of fieldwork in an unfamiliar setting; on the other, it denied us the intimacy of participant observation common to anthropologists who work in village settings. As it turned out, this separation gave me a neutrality which preserved the opportunity for future research. If we had made a commitment to reside with a particular family during this first field trip, it might have adversely curtailed our future options.

Studying a Dispersed Population

When I arrived in Mexico City, I had a list of about twenty migrants' names and just two addresses, which I had obtained in a hurried search through Foster's data files before my departure from Berkeley. My immediate goal was to locate as many migrants as possible, as quickly as I could, so that I might get on with the real fieldwork. It took me about a year to slowly develop a social network which included nearly all of the migrants; in fact, my network became so much wider than that of any of the Tzintzuntzeños that they used to ask me where one of their fellows lived or worked. Having to go from household to household made me aware of the importance of the Tzintzuntzeños' mutual assistance arrangements with kinsmen, other ex-villagers, and other urban residents; I came to appreciate first-hand the impact of urban distances on the social and economic situations of people without cars or phones; and I eventually realized why the migrants seemed to lack a sense of "community."

Collecting Field Data

Following Foster's example, I adopted the widely-used HRAF system for coding and filing field notes. Information was typed onto 5 x 8 inch sheets and filed in two sets: one arranged topically in the HRAF numerical categories; the other by households. A third copy was mailed periodically to Berkeley, where Foster read the notes, wrote comments to me regarding points of special interest, and then filed them for safekeeping.

The most important element common to our research efforts was the 1970 ethnographic census. We asked for almost identical information and gave the census at about the same time. Whereas Foster was able to obtain a 100% response rate in the village, I censused only about 70% (51 of 74 household units) of the migrants first-hand. Although in nearly all of the remaining cases I was able to get reliable second-hand information, I knew that circumstances in the city made a 100% census virtually impossible.

In retrospect, it is fortunate that I did my initial fieldwork among the migrants at the same time that Foster was administering a census in the village. Because of this coincidence, I now have a good set of demographic and socioeconomic "core" data on the Tzintzuntzeños in the capital and in the home community. Moreover, because the Mexican government conducted its decennial national census in February 1970, I can relate the ethnographic census data for Tzintzuntzan migrants and villagers to the broader regional and national situation.

FIELDWORK IN 1974

The most important aspect of the summer 1974 field season was that I accomplished almost as much in ten weeks as I had before in as many months. The "costs" of the research, both in money and personal effort, were substantially reduced during this second field trip. Not only did I know much more about the population I was studying, I was also a more mature, more effective ethnographer.

Selecting a Place to Live

On this occasion I went alone to Mexico City and lived with a migrant family. This particular family had been our closest friends among the migrants in 1969 and 1970; furthermore, the household head was the half-brother of the woman in whose home Foster lives while in Tzintzuntzan. They thus had a good idea of the needs of an anthropologist and were willing to attend to mine. In short, the situation was ideal for getting maximum work done in a short time.

More important than having a place to live was the chance to observe first-hand on a daily basis the interpersonal relationships within a migrant home. In addition, the family's entrepreneurship (they had opened two small stores) gave me an insider's view of how migrants try to improve their economic situation in the city. And, finally, the family served as willing key informants on a wide range of topics. Since the family and I both are pleased with the arrangement, it appears that I have a place to which I can always return while doing fieldwork.

Studying a Dispersed Population

Based on my earlier fieldwork, I knew that it would be impossible, in ten weeks or in a hundred, to locate and survey every Tzintzuntzan migrant in Mexico City. I did hope to canvass, with some field assistance, about 75% of the population; in fact, we were able to gather first-hand data on more than 70 households and got reliable second-hand data on most of the remainder out of a total of about 105 households.

Since I had no car on this field trip, I depended on the excellent public transportation system of taxis, jitney cabs, buses, and subways. In addition, the family with whom I lived took me to visit other migrant households on weekends and in their spare time. The large number of recent arrivals forced a strict rationing of time and effort. That also forced me to visit Tzintzuntzan to check on the dozen or so "return migrants" and to ascertain who else had left the village since the 1970 census. In the process, I confirmed the emigration of villagers to Mexico City and also to many other destinations, including the United States.

For studying a dispersed population, a series of visits has many advantages. This time I knew what faced me and how to plan my available time to see as many migrants as possible. I did not have to build a social network family by family; I already had one which enabled me to cope with the migrants' geographical distribution in the metropolis. Moreover, the second visit to the Tzintzuntzeños made me aware of continuities and changes which I had not observed on the first field trip.

Changing Roles in the Field

Previously I had been a student, now I was a professor. Nevertheless, because of my age (28), I continued to introduce myself as "Roberto" and asked that people so address me. I continued to use the formal *"Usted"* rather than the informal *"tu"* in all conversations except with age mates (and children) whom I knew well and who used it first in speaking with me.

When I had been a student, I could plead poverty when unusual requests for assistance arose. Now this was more difficult, and as I continue the research my social debts to the migrants and villagers will have to be repaid with interest. Additional burdens of reciprocity also accrue with professional colleagues in Mexico City. As an anthropologist hoping to carry out research in Mexico for the rest of my career, I feel responsible to lecture in local universities, to publish papers and books in Spanish in local journals and monograph series, and to assist in training local students. This is an obligation I incur in exchange for the privilege of continuing my fieldwork.

PERSONAL DIMENSIONS OF LONG-TERM RESEARCH

I feel a considerable personal investment in the fieldwork among the Tzintzuntzan migrants in Mexico City. As a partner in reciprocal relationships, I believe that I have a responsibility to assist them (within my limited resources) in exchange for their continuing cooperation in my research. The migrants are generally literate, highly motivated, and hard-working; they are as colleagues in a common research enterprise, not laboratory subjects upon whom instruments are tested. And even when a few of them refuse to talk with me, I respect their desire for privacy.

I have good friends among both the older and younger Tzintzun- tzeños in Mexico City. Within a decade or so, many of these people will be pensioned, while others will reach middle age. This demographic shift will occur as I, too, grow older. It is likely that an interest in life cycles and in the development cycles of domestic groups will become important in my future research as I begin to work among the second and third generation of Tzintzuntzeños in the capital.

THEORETICAL AND METHODOLOGICAL CONSIDERATIONS

Nearly all studies of urbanization conducted by anthropologists have stressed the "community" as a natural unit of analysis. The dispersion of the Tzintzuntzan migrants in metropolitan Mexico City suggests that populations also can be studied in "non-place" situations. This raises the issue: who or what are we studying in long-term research? And how long is sufficient to conduct research among particular groups? In my case, I have taken a pragmatic stance. The unit of analysis is the set of persons affiliated with households in which Tzintzuntzan migrants reside. The period of research is three decades, which seems long enough to describe intergenerational mobility. In sum, my definition of the problem to be studied is rather open-ended in the belief that this minimizes the chance of missing important data.

Ultimately, the signal advantage of long-term research on urbanization is that no amount of cross-sectional research yields satisfying diachronic results. Slices of time, no matter how carefully selected, fail to attain the richness of field materials drawn from repeated visits among a well studied population. These statements will not surprise many economists, psychologists, or political scientists; panel studies have long been a principal component in their methodological repertoires. Anthropologists lately come to urban research are only beginning to explore the merits of short-term and long-term studies. The decisions made now will influence the quality and quantity of our contributions to comparative urban theory for years ahead.

FIG. A-1—The author interviewing a migrant at a house located on the northern periphery of Mexico City.

Fieldwork among the Tzintzuntzan migrants suggests that anthropologists should not undertake a long-term study without developing or building upon a strong data base from which subsequent changes can be measured. When considering the investment of time and effort in long-term research, perhaps anthropologists might employ an approach used by many archaeologists: survey potential field sites, assess the merits and demerits of each site, conduct preliminary fieldwork in the most promising sites, perform initial data analysis, and then decide where further research is justified. But, in contrast to archaeologists, social anthropologists seem to have few guidelines to tell them when enough fieldwork has been done in a particular place.

So long as individual fieldworkers are the primary agents of anthropological research, their ability to establish rapport and maintain good relations with particular populations will be the foundation of long-term field projects. They will have to be aware of their own changing professional and personal development—and be able to continue field research in the face of changing family circumstances, jobs, health, and theoretical inclinations. And they will have to be sufficiently productive as scholars to garner continuing support for their field research from funding agencies and from their social science colleagues. The value of any long-term study, whether among the Tzintzuntzan migrants in Mexico City or among the Eskimo, will not be fully measured in the short run. Long after today's theoretical fads and methodological innovations have been tossed aside, the data collected carefully and patiently over several decades in key ethnographic settings will continue to provide a basis for testing new ideas.

REFERENCES CITED

ARIZPE, L., 1976. "Migración indígena, problemas analíticos." Nueva Antropología 2(5):63-89.

BALAN, J., 1969. "Migrant-Native Socioeconomic Differences in Latin American Cities: A Structural Analysis." Latin American Research Review 4(1):3-29.

―――, H. BROWNING, and E. JELIN, 1973. Men in a Developing Society: Geographic and Social Mobility in Monterrey, Mexico. (Latin American Monographs, No. 30, Institute of Latin American Studies.) Austin: The University of Texas Press.

BENDER, D., 1967. "A Refinement of the Concept of Household: Families, Co-Residence, and Domestic Functions." American Anthropologist 69(5):493-504.

BONILLA, F., 1964. "The Urban Worker." In John J. Johnson (ed.), Continuity and Change in Latin America, pp. 186-205. Stanford, Calif.: Stanford University Press.

BRANDES, S., 1975. Migration, Kinship, and Community: Tradition and Transition in a Spanish Village. New York: Academic Press.

BRODY, E., 1969. "Migration and Adaptation: The Nature of the Problem." In E. Brody (ed.), Behavior in New Environments, pp. 14-21. Beverly Hills, Calif.: Sage Publications.

BROWN J., 1972. Patterns of Intra-Urban Settlement in Mexico City: An Examination of the Turner Theory. (Latin American Studies Program, Dissertation Series No. 40.) Ithaca: Cornell University.

BROWNING, H., 1971. "Migrant Selectivity and the Growth of Large Cities in Developing Societies." In National Academy of Sciences (ed.), Rapid Population Growth, pp. 273-314. Baltimore: Johns Hopkins Press.

――, and W. FEINDT, 1969. "Selectivity of Migrants to a Metropolis in a Developing Country: A Mexican Case Study." Demography 6(4):347-357.

――, and W. FEINDT, 1971. "Patterns of Migration to Monterrey, Mexico." The International Migration Review 5(3):309-324.

BUECHLER, H., 1975. "Comments." In B. Du Toit and H. Safa (eds.), Migration and Urbanization: Models and Adaptive Strategies, pp. 285-289. The Hague: Mouton.

BUTTERWORTH, D., 1962. "A Study of the Urbanization Process among Mixtec Migrants from Tilantongo in Mexico City." América Indígena 22(3):257-274.

――, 1969. Factors in Out-Migration from a Rural Mexican Community. Unpublished Ph.D. dissertation (University Microfilms No. 70-806). Urbana: University of Illinois.

――, 1971. "Migración rural-urbana en América Latina: el estado de nuestro conocimiento." América Indígena 31(1):85-106.

CARDONA, R. and A. SIMMONS, 1975. "Toward a Model of Migration in Latin America." In B. Du Toit and H. Safa (eds.), Migration and Urbanization: Models and Adaptive Strategies, pp. 19-48. The Hague: Mouton.

CARLOS, M. and L. SELLERS, 1972. "Family, Kinship Structure, and Modernization in Latin America." Latin American Research Review 7(2):95-124.

C.E.E.D. (Centro de Estudios Económicos y Demográficos), 1970. Dinámica de la población de México. México, D.F.: El Colegio de México.

CEPAL (Comision Económica para América Latina), 1975. Población y Desarrollo en América Latina. México, D.F.: Fondo de Cultura Económica.

CHANCE, J., 1971. "Kinship and Urban Residence: Household and Family Organization in a Suburb of Oaxaca, Mexico." Journal of the Steward Anthropological Society 2:122-147.

CLINE, H., 1963. Mexico: Revolution to Evolution: 1940–1960. New York: Oxford University Press.

CORNELIUS, W., 1974. "Introduction." In W. Cornelius and F. True-blood (eds.), Anthropological Perspectives on Latin American Urbanization pp. 9-20. (Latin American Urban Research Vol. 4.) Beverly Hills, Calif.: Sage Publications.

–––, 1975. Politics and the Migrant Poor in Mexico City. Stanford, Calif.: Stanford University Press.

CORONA RENTERIA, A., 1974. La economía urbana: ciudades y regiones mexicanas. México, D.F.: Instituto Mexicano de Investigaciones Económicas.

CORWIN, A., 1963. Contemporary Mexican Attitudes toward Population, Poverty, and Public Opinion. Gainesville: University of Florida Press.

DE RIDDER, J., 1960. The Personality of the Urban African in South Africa. London: Routledge and Kegan Paul, International Library of Sociology and Social Reconstruction.

DU TOIT, B. 1975. "Introduction: Migration and Population Mobility." In B. Du Toit and H. Safa (eds.), Migration and Urbanization: Models and Adaptive Strategies, pp. 1-15. The Hague: Mouton.

ESTEVA FABREGAT, C., 1969. "Familia y matrimonio en México: el patrón cultural." Revista de Indias 115-118:173-278.

FOSTER, G., 1965. "Peasant Society and the Image of Limited Good." American Anthropologist 67:293-315.

–––, 1967. Tzintzuntzan: Mexican Peasants in a Changing World. Boston: Little, Brown & Co.

———, 1969. "Godparents and Social Networks in Tzintzuntzan." Southwestern Journal of Anthropology 25(3):261-278.

———, 1972. "A Second Look at Limited Good." Anthropological Quarterly 45:57-64.

———, and G. OSPINA, 1948. Empire's Children: The People of Tzintzuntzan. Mexico, D.F.: Smithsonian Institution, Institute of Social Anthropology, Publication No. 6.

FRIED, M., 1969. "Deprivation and Migration." In E. Brody (ed.), Behavior in New Environments, pp. 23-72. Beverly Hills, Calif.: Sage Publications.

GERMANI, G., 1961. "Inquiry into the Social Effects of Urbanization in a Working-Class Sector of Greater Buenos Aires." In Philip M. Hauser (ed.), Urbanization in Latin America, pp. 159-178. New York: UNESCO.

———, 1967. "The City as an Integrating Mechanism." In Glenn H. Beyer (ed.), The Urban Explosion in Latin America, pp. 175-214. Ithaca: Cornell University Press.

GONZALEZ, N., 1965. "The Consanguineal Household and Matrifocality." American Anthropologist 67(6):1541-1549.

———, 1969. Black Carib Household Structure: A Study of Migration and Modernization. Seattle and London: University of Washington Press.

GOODE, J., 1970. "Latin American Urbanism and Corporate Groups." Anthropological Quarterly 43:146-167.

GRAVES, N. and T. GRAVES, 1974. "Adaptive Strategies in Urban Migration." In B. J. Siegel (ed.), Annual Review of Anthropology, Vol. 3, pp. 117-152. Palo Alto, Calif.: Annual Reviews, Inc.

GRAVES, T., 1966. "Alternative Models for the Study of Urban Migration." Human Organization 25(4):295-300.

GUILLET, D. and D. UZZELL (eds.), 1976. New Approaches to the Study of Migration. Houston: Rice University Studies: Vol. 62, No. 3.

GULLIVER, P., 1971. Neighbours and Networks: The Idiom of Kinship in Social Action among the Ndendeuli of Tanzania. Berkeley, Los Angeles, London: University of California Press.

HANSON, R. and O. SIMMONS, 1968. "The Role Path: A Concept and Procedure for Studying Migration to Urban Communities." Human Organization 27(2):152-158.

HERRICK, B., 1965. Urban Migration and Economic Development in Chile. Cambridge: The M.I.T. Press.

JACKSON, H., 1973. "Intra-Urban Migration of Mexico City's Poor." Ph.D. in Geography dissertation, University of Colorado. (Xerox University Microfilms Order No. 73-23,260.)

KAHL, J., 1968. The Measurement of Modernism: A Study of Values in Brazil and Mexico. (Latin American Monograph Series No. 12.) Austin: University of Texas Press.

KEMPER, R., 1974. "Tzintzuntzeños in Mexico City; The Anthropologist among Peasant Migrants." In George M. Foster and Robert V. Kemper (eds.), Anthropologists in Cities, pp. 63-91. Boston: Little, Brown & Co.

———, and G. FOSTER, 1975. "Urbanization in Mexico: The View from Tzintzuntzan." In W. A. Cornelius and F. M. Trueblood (eds.), Urbanization and Inequality: The Political Economy of Urban and Rural Development in Latin America (Latin American Urban Research, Vol. 5), pp. 53-75. Beverly Hills, Calif. and London: Sage Publications.

LAJOUS VARGAS, A., 1968. "Aspectos regionales de la expansión de la educación superior en México, 1959–1967." Demografía y Economía 2(3):404-427.

LEEDS, A. and E. LEEDS, 1970. "Brazil and the Myth of Urban Ru-
rality: Urban Experience, Work and Values in 'Squatments' of Rio
de Janiero and Lima." In Arthur J. Field (ed.), City and Country in
the Third World, pp. 229-285. Cambridge: Schenkman.

LEÑERO OTERO, L., 1968. Investigación de la familia en México.
México, D.F.: Instituto Mexicano de Estudios Sociales, A.C.

LEWIS, O., 1952. "Urbanization without Breakdown: A Case Study."
The Scientific Monthly 75:31-41.

———, 1959. Five Families: Mexican Case Studies in the Culture of
Poverty. New York: Basic Books.

———, 1965. "Further Observations on the Folk-Urban Continuum and
Urbanization with Special Reference to Mexico City." In Philip M.
Hauser and Leo Schnore (eds.), The Study of Urbanization, pp.
491-503. New York: John Wiley & Sons.

L. M. S., 1968. "El D.F. y la provincia." Examen de la Situación
Económica de México 44(514):11-15.

LOMNITZ, L. DE, 1975. Como sobreviven los marginados. México,
D.F.: Siglo XXI Editores, S.A.

MANGIN, W., 1967. "Latin American Squatter Settlements: A Problem and a Solution." Latin American Research Review 2(3):65-98.

MC GEE, T., 1975. "Malay Migration to Kuala Lumpur City: Individual
Adaptation to the City." In B. Du Toit and H. Safa (eds.), Migration
and Urbanization: Models and Adaptive Strategies, pp. 143-178. The
Hague: Mouton.

MENDEZ, E., 1970. "Las telecomunicaciones." In Instituto de Investigaciones Sociales (ed.), El Perfil de México en 1980, Vol. 2, pp.
119-167. México, D.F.: Siglo XXI Editores, S.A.

MIDGETT, D., 1976. "Conceptual Problems in Migration Studies."
Journal of the Steward Anthropological Society 7(2):253-273.

NAVARRETE, I., 1970. "La Distribución del ingreso en México: tendencias y perspectivas." In David Ibarra, Ifigenia M. de Navarrete, Leopoldo Solis M., and Victor L. Urquid, El Perfil de México en 1980, Vol. 1, pp. 15-71. México, D.F.: Siglo XXI Editores, S.A.

NELSON, C., 1971. The Waiting Village: Social Change in Rural Mexico. Boston: Little, Brown & Co.

NUTINI, H., 1967. "A Synoptic Comparison of Mesoamerican Marriage and Family Structure." Southwestern Journal of Anthropology 23(4):383-404.

———, 1976. "Demographic Functions of Compadrazgo in Santa Maria Belen Azitzimititlan and Rural Tlaxcala." In H. Nutini (ed.), Essays on Mexican Kinship, pp. 219-236. Pittsburgh: University of Pittsburgh Press.

OLIVEIRA, O. DE, and C. STERN, 1974. "Notas acerca de la teoría de las migraciones internas: aspectos sociológicos." In H. Muñoz et al., Las migraciones internas en América Latina, pp. 59-82. Buenos Aires: Ediciones Nueva Vision (Fichas No. 38).

PATCH, R., 1961. Life in a Callejón: A Study of Urban Disorganization. American Universities Field Staff, West Coast South America Series 8, 6.

PEATTIE, L., 1968. The View from the Barrio. Ann Arbor: University of Michigan Press.

RAVENSTEIN, E., 1885. "The Laws of Migration." Journal of the Royal Statistical Society 48(2):167-227.

ROBERTS, B., 1970. "The Social Organization of Low-Income Families." In Irving Louis Horowitz (ed.), Masses in Latin America, pp. 345-382. New York: Oxford University Press.

ROTONDO, H. et al., 1963. "Personalidad básica, dilemas y vida de familia de un grupo de mestizos." In Baltazar Caravedo, Humberto Rotondo, and Javier Mariategui (eds.), Estudios de Psiquiatría Social en el Péru, pp. 208-262. Lima: Ediciones del Sol.

SAFA, H., 1964. "From Shanty Town to Public Housing: A Comparison of Family Structure in Two Urban Neighborhoods in Puerto Rico." Caribbean Studies 4(1):3-12.

SAUERS, B., 1974. "Peasant Migrations in Latin America: A Survey of the Literature in English." Peasant Studies Newsletter 3(2): 19-26.

SECRETARIA DE INDUSTRIA y COMERCIO, 1971. IX Censo General de Población, 1970: Resumen General. México, D.F.: Talleres Gráficos de la Nación.

SHANNON, L., and M. SHANNON, 1968. "The Assimilation of Migrants to Cities: Anthropological and Sociological Contributions." In L. Schnore (ed.), Social Science and the City: A Survey of Urban Research, pp. 49-75. New York: Frederick A. Praeger.

SHAW, R., 1975. Migration Theory and Fact: A Review and Bibliography of Current Literature. Philadelphia: Regional Science Research Institute.

SIMMONS, O.; R. HANSON; and R. POTTER, 1967. The Rural Migrant in the Urban World of Work. Manuscript. Published in Proceedings of the IX Inter-American Congress of Psychology.

SINGER, P., 1973. "Migraciones internas en América Latina: consideraciones teóricas sobre su estudio." In M. Castells (ed.), Imperialismo y Urbanización en América Latina, pp. 27-56. Barcelona: Editorial Gustavo Gili.

SWARTZBAUGH, R., 1970. Machismo: A Value System of a Mexican Peasant Class. Ph.D. dissertation. Ohio State University (University Microfilms 70-14,104).

TAEUBER, K.; L. CHIAZZE, JR.; and W. HAENZEL, 1968. Migration in the United States: An Analysis of Residence Histories. Washington, D.C.: U. S. Department of Health, Education, and Welfare, Public Health Monograph No. 77.

TOOMEY, D., 1970. "The Importance of Social Networks in Working-Class Areas." Urban Studies 7:259-270.

TURNER, J., 1965. "Lima's Barriadas and Corralones: Suburbs versus Slums." Ekistics 19(12):152-155.

———, 1967. "Barriers and Channels for Housing Development in Modernizing Countries." Journal of the American Institute of Planners 33(3):167-181.

———, 1968. "Housing Priorities, Settlement Patterns, and Urban Development in Modernizing Countries." Journal of the American Institute of Planners 34(6):354-363.

UNIKEL, L., 1971. "La dinámica del crecimiento de la ciudad de México." Comercio Exterior 21(6):507-516.

———, and A. NECOCHEA, 1971. "Jerarquía y sistema de ciudades en México." Demografía y Economía 5(1):27-39.

UNITED NATIONS, 1971. Demographic Yearbook—1970. New York: Department of Social and Economic Affairs, Statistical Office of the United Nations.

WEAVER, T., and T. DOWNING (eds.), 1976. Mexican Migration. Tucson: Bureau of Ethnic Research, Department of Anthropology, University of Arizona.

WHITEFORD, M., 1976. The Forgotten Ones: Colombian Countrymen in an Urban Setting. Gainesville: The University of Florida Press. (Latin American Monographs, Second Series, No. 20.)

WILKIE, J., 1974. "Mexico City as a Magnet for Mexico's Economically Active Population, 1930–1965." In J. Wilkie, Statistics and National Policy, pp. 41-51. (Statistical Abstract of Latin America, Supplement 3.) Los Angeles: UCLA Latin American Center.

WOLF, E., 1966. "Kinship, Friendship and Patron-Client Relations in Complex Societies." In Michael Banton (ed.), The Social Anthropology of Complex Societies, pp. 1-22. London: Tavistock.

ABOUT THE AUTHOR

ROBERT V. KEMPER is an Associate Professor of Anthropology at Southern Methodist University. He received his Ph.D. from the University of California (Berkeley) in 1971. He is Associate Editor of two major journals in the field of urban studies: *Urban Anthropology* and *Comparative Urban Research*. Among his principal publications are: *Anthropologists in Cities* (with George M. Foster—Little, Brown, 1974); *Campesinos en la ciudad: gente de Tzintzuntzan* (Ediciones SepSetentas, Mexico City, 1976); *Metropolitan Problems and Governmental Responses in Latin America* (co-editor with Wayne A. Cornelius—Sage Publications, 1977); *The History of Anthropology: A Research Bibliography* (with John F. S. Phinney—Garland, 1977); and *Many Happy Returns: The Theoretical and Methodological Implications of Long-Term Field Research in Social Anthropology* (with Elizabeth Colson, George M. Foster, and Thayer Scudder—forthcoming). In addition to his interests in Mexico and comparative urbanization theories, he recently began research on the impact of tourism on regional development in northern New Mexico and southern California. Professor Kemper is a Fellow of the American Anthropological Association, the Society for Applied Anthropology, and the American Association for the Advancement of Science.